BEASTS

BY THE SAME AUTHOR

Dogs Make Us Human

The Interpretation of Dreams by Sigmund Freud
(ed. with an introduction and essays by J. M. Masson)

The Dog Who Couldn't Stop Loving

The Face on Your Plate

Altruistic Armadillos, Zenlike Zebras

Raising the Peaceable Kingdom

Slipping into Paradise

The Cat Who Came in from the Cold

The Pig Who Sang to the Moon

The Nine Emotional Lives of Cats

The Emperor's Embrace

Dogs Have the Strangest Friends

Dogs Never Lie About Love

Lost Prince

When Elephants Weep

Kaspar Hauser

My Father's Guru

Final Analysis

Against Therapy

A Dark Science

The Assault on Truth

The Complete Letters of Sigmund Freud to Wilhelm Fliess 1887–1904
(tr. and ed.)

Santarasa and Abhinavagupta's Philosophy of Aesthetics
(with M. V. Patwardhan)

Avimaraka (with D. D. Kosambi)

Aesthetic Rapture

The Oceanic Feeling

Love Poems from the Ancient Sanskrit (with W. S. Merwin)

The Dhvanyaloka of Anandavardhana with the Locana of Abhinavagupta
(tr. by Daniel H. H. Ingalls, J. M. Masson, and M. V. Patwardhan; ed.
and with an introduction by Daniel H. H. Ingalls)

BEASTS

What Animals Can Teach Us About Human Nature

JEFFREY MOUSSAIEFF MASSON

B L O O M S B U R Y

LONDON · NEW DELHI · NEW YORK · SYDNEY

Bloomsbury Publishing Plc
50 Bedford Square
London
WC1B 3DP

www.bloomsbury.com

Bloomsbury is a trade mark of Bloomsbury Publishing Plc

Bloomsbury Publishing, London, New Delhi, New York and Sydney

A CIP catalogue record for this book is available from the British Library

ISBN 978 1 4088 1876 3

10 9 8 7 6 5 4 3 2 1

Typeset by Hewer Text UK Ltd, Edinburgh
Printed and bound in Great Britain by CPI Group (UK) Ltd, Croydon CR0 4YY

For Leila and Terri
and for our children—Ilan, Manu, and Simone—
and to my friend Daniel Ellsberg

Swimming the ocean a giant brain watches us.
  —Jeffrey Moussaieff Masson

Contents

PREFACE: CAN THE HUMAN SPECIES WAKE UP?

We only have to look at ourselves to see how intelligent life might develop into something we wouldn't want to meet.

—Stephen Hawking

TOO OFTEN WE HEAR PEOPLE SAY of somebody, "He is a beast!" meaning that the person's behavior is awful, dangerous, violent, cruel. The word *animal* is used the same way. And yet in my research I have been struck over and over by how far off this characterization is. Beasts— or any animal except the human animal—have few of the failings we, as a species, have. It is one of the great conundrums of our time. How is it that, with our advanced intelligence, humans are far behind almost every other animal when it comes to living in harmony with their own nature and with nature? Humans make terrible distinctions about one another; other animals do not.

Many years ago, I was hiking in southern Italy when I came to a small village where I got to chatting with one of the locals. He was telling me, sadly, that his son had married a *stranieri*, a foreigner. She was from far away, he explained. Intrigued, I asked what country she was from. "She is from the next village, a full five miles down the road," he answered.

Since that time I have wondered what it is specifically about humans that makes us fail to recognize that all of us belong to a single species, even though we most certainly do. As any geneticist will tell you, any two humans are more genetically similar than a lowland gorilla and a mountain gorilla. But this is not something obvious to us. Quite the contrary. E. O. Wilson, in *The Social Conquest of Earth*, claims, "Tribal conflict, where believers on the inside were pitted against infidels on the outside, was a principal driving force that shaped biological human nature."[1] It is as if we are doomed to making a permanent distinction between "us" and "them." Warfare, it has been claimed, is endemic to our species. Even President Obama, in his Nobel Peace Prize acceptance speech, echoed this widespread belief: "War in one form or another appeared with the first man." He is, in my opinion, badly mistaken.[2]

Science has now admitted both the mental and emotional continuities between humans and other animals. Since Darwin first wrote about this more than 150 years ago, there has been a veritable Everest of scientific data, not to mention personal experience, attesting to animal sentience and how similar humans and animals are, even at the genetic level. Why, then, do humans persist in self-destructive violent behavior atypical of the animal kingdom? Human understanding has not translated into a change in behavior. While we are perhaps the only animal* willing to risk our lives for the sake of an animal from a completely different species (consider how people will rush into a burning building to save their pet dog, cat, or even bird), we are *also* the animal that displays the most violence toward its own kind. However, I believe that

---

* Meaning animals under natural conditions in the wild; this does not include dogs, about which more later.

examining the more peaceable nature of other large-brained mammals—even the predators, the ones we call beasts—may point the way to a more peaceable existence for all.

The two main predators on the planet—humans, on land, and orcas, in the oceans—are similar in a number of ways. Both have enormous brains. Both have culture, that is, both species pass on information to their young through learning. This is true of other species as well, but humans and orcas take this further than any other animal. Both hunt in groups; both have sophisticated communication skills. Both live a long life and are enormously social. Both have the us/them distinction. But whereas we use this us/them to murder untold millions of our fellow humans, orcas have never killed a single one of their own species, as far as anyone has been able to ascertain.[3] We are special, especially bad—but also good, as I will show—when compared to all the other predators. Not only are we bad to our fellow humans, but we are bad to other species. Many other predators kill one another only in very small numbers, if at all; even more important, in contrast to humans, they kill other animals exclusively out of necessity, to eat them. We kill orcas, and all other animals, sometimes to eat them, though we have no need to eat them, and also just for the hell of it.[4] What happened to us as a species that we are so different?

Greed has become unmoored from any real need, just as eating and fighting seem to have become similarly unmoored. Early on in our species's history, fighting was ritualized, that is, it was not deadly. But that changed. Other animals would never take the kinds of chances we do that put us in harm's way (warfare, for example); it makes no evolutionary sense. Only we create artificial and arbitrary distinctions—different race; different language; different religion—for which we are willing to kill and die. This is not true of any other animal, as far as anyone has been able to establish.

The use of our extraordinary intellectual power has become

disconnected from our needs as well, so it works not to make us safe but to expose us to ever greater dangers. I will argue in this book that this process began with the domestication of animals, which has brought to the fore a latent cruelty in humans. (The stock market is so called because originally our wealth was in livestock.) In the past, finding and killing an animal was a rare and dangerous occasion, circumscribed by tradition, superstitions, and rituals; now it has become routine and ugly—witness any of the undercover videos of slaughterhouse activity that *nobody* wants to see. It is not surprising that some researchers believe that the men who engage in this job are among the most stressed workers in the world, the unhappiest, and the ones with the greatest propensity toward domestic violence.[5] This could not possibly be how we were meant to interact with the other animals who share the planet.

Richard Alexander, one of the founders of evolutionary biology, tells me that the greatest difficulty in seeking global harmony may derive from human groups targeting one another. Humans alone among all the world's species plot, plan, and organize massive conflicts to defeat or displace similarly organized members of their own species.

Is it possible that we are living as traumatized beings? It could well be. Consider the elephants Gay Bradshaw describes in *Elephants on the Edge: What Animals Teach Us about Humanity*. Normally elephants do not callously, cruelly, and needlessly kill other animals. But recently scientists report seeing young bull elephants doing precisely that with rhinos, and not only killing them but raping them as well (much as human soldiers do in war). What turned them into psychopathic killers? Bradshaw examines evidence that trauma, in this case seeing their mothers murdered in front of their eyes when they were still little, is the cause. I cover this in the epilogue to this book, but I think our entire species may be experiencing something similar. Our hyperviolence could be at least partially explained by a traumatic past. More on this later.

What could awaken us from this self-imposed trance of destruction? Seeking the answers I pursue in this book is not an idle quest. I do it in the hope that we can change.

1 · Crocodiles and Us

This concept of human identity positions humans outside and above the food chain, not as part of the feast in a chain of reciprocity but as external manipulators and masters of it: Animals can be our food, but we can never be their food. The outrage we experience at the idea of a human being eaten is certainly not what we experience at the idea of animals as food.

—Valerie Plumwood

 VALERIE PLUMWOOD, A PROMINENT ECOFEMINIST WHO taught at the University of Montana and the University of Sydney, wrote in *Feminism and the Mastery of Nature* about what she called the "hyperseparation" between the self and others, especially other animals. Her view is that by setting humans up as masters of nature we have manipulated ourselves into becoming a species of warriors, at war with other species, rather than simply coexisting with them:

The idea of human prey threatens the dualistic vision of human mastery in which we humans manipulate nature from outside, as predators but never prey. We may daily consume other animals by the billions, but we ourselves cannot be food for worms and certainly not meat for crocodiles. This is one reason why we now treat so inhumanely the animals we make our food, for we cannot imagine ourselves similarly positioned as food. We act as if we live in a separate realm of culture in which we are never food, while other animals inhabit a different world of nature in which they are no more than food, and their lives can be utterly distorted in the service of this end.[1]

Plumwood believes we are misguided to view ourselves as controllers of a tamed and malleable natural world, as she puts it, with no more violent beasts for us to overcome. If this self-assessment bears any relation to the truth, moreover, it is only because *we* have become the violent beast. Instead of having other animals in our jaws, we have one another. We also perpetrate mass violence against our own kind. Warfare is organized fighting, which involves a willingness to submit to authority, a risk of injury and death, and premeditation, and it has lethal violence at its heart.

Waging war has become a bad habit; other people do it and encourage us to try it. We have become so accustomed to it that we find it normal. In some sense, it defines us as a species: we are the animal who is engaged in near-constant warfare. Do animals engage in anything like this?

Consider the crocodile. In 1985, something happened to Valerie Plumwood that is relevant to this discussion. She was in Kakadu National Park, near Darwin, in the Australian Northern Territories.[2] She was alone in a small canoe in a place called East Alligator Lagoon (an odd name for a country that does not have alligators), looking for caves with indigenous rock art. She had been warned by the rangers that there were many crocodiles in these remote waters and that she should not be gone long or stray too far. Under no circumstances must she enter the main river.

For hours she searched the maze of shallow channels in the swamp but did not find the channel leading to the rock art site. Rather than return defeated, she decided to explore a clear, deep channel closer to the river. But the channel only led back again to the main river, the very place she had been warned not to enter. She began to think she should have sought the advice of the original owners of Kakadu, the indigenous Gagadju. They would have told her to stay away.

Plumwood had the sensation of being watched.

She became intensely aware of the precariousness of her own life—indeed, of human lives in general: "As a solitary specimen of a major prey species of the saltwater crocodile, I was standing in one of the most dangerous places on earth."* We are just another animal, prey sometimes, predator at others. But humans are not used to being seen as prey. That is why her account is so profound.

Perhaps lulled by the magical beauty of the birds and the water lilies, she did proceed into the main river. Ten minutes downstream, she noticed what she thought was a floating stick. But it developed eyes. It was no stick; it was a crocodile. "How interesting," was her first thought, like a tourist being shown the local wildlife from the safety of a boat. But her little canoe was not safe. Suddenly, the crocodile rammed it hard, coming at it over and over. She had the stark realization: "I am prey." There can be no more horrible thought. She made the split-second decision to leap into the branches of a large tree growing on the bank of the river, knowing her only chance of escape was if she could make it into the tree. She stood up, ready to jump from the canoe.

---

* I am not sure why she says that we are a major prey species of the crocodile. As far as I know, and experts agree, this is not so. There usually are no more than one or two human deaths from crocodiles per year in Australia.

At the same instant, the crocodile rushed up alongside the canoe, and its beautiful, flecked golden eyes looked straight into mine. Perhaps I could bluff it, drive it away, as I had read of British tiger hunters doing. I waved my arms and shouted, "Go away!" (We're British here.) The golden eyes glinted with interest. I tensed for the jump and leapt. Before my foot even tripped the first branch, I had a blurred, incredulous vision of great toothed jaws bursting from the water. Then I was seized between the legs in a red-hot pincer grip and whirled into the suffocating wet darkness.

At that instant, Plumwood's world was turned topsy-turvy. She told herself that this could not be happening, that it was a nightmare from which she would soon awake. "This desperate delusion split apart as I hit the water. In that flash, I glimpsed the world for the first time 'from the outside,' as a world no longer my own, an unrecognizable bleak landscape composed of raw necessity, indifferent to my life or death."

Worse was to come, for the crocodile did what crocodiles do when wanting to subdue prey. Few of those who have experienced the crocodile's death roll have lived to describe it. It was, for Plumwood, "essentially, an experience beyond words," one "of total terror." She knew that

the crocodile's breathing and heart metabolism are not suited to prolonged struggle, so the roll is an intense burst of power designed to overcome the victim's resistance quickly. The crocodile then holds the feebly struggling prey underwater until it drowns. The roll was a centrifuge of boiling blackness that lasted for an eternity, beyond endurance, but when I seemed all but finished, the rolling suddenly stopped. My feet touched bottom, my head broke the surface, and, coughing, I sucked at air, amazed to be alive. The crocodile still had me in its pincer grip between the legs.

But it was not over: "I had just begun to weep for the prospects of my mangled body when the crocodile pitched me suddenly into a second death roll."

She survived this second bout of whirling and surfaced, still in the crocodile's grip, next to a branch of a large sandpaper fig tree growing in the water. She grabbed the branch, vowing to let the crocodile tear her apart rather than throw her again into that spinning, suffocating hell. But when she tried to climb into the tree, the crocodile seized her again, this time around the upper left thigh, and pulled her under for a third time. When she resurfaced she was again near the tree branch. She was able to hoist herself up, and then, inexplicably, the crocodile suddenly let go of her thigh and she was able to reach the muddy bank above the tree. (Crocodiles tire easily, and this was his third attempt at subduing this stubborn woman.)

Plumwood was so exhausted, however, and the bank was so slippery, that she began to slide down toward the waiting jaws. She jammed her fingers into the mud and was able to pull herself forward. Her life depended on doing this a few more times, and she did. Severely wounded, bleeding profusely, and in a driving rainstorm, she managed to crawl two miles through mosquito-infested tropical swamps, losing consciousness several times before being found by the ranger who had warned her of the dangers of the river in the first place. The nurses who attended her in the hospital say her injuries were among the worst they had ever seen. So I cannot entertain the hypothesis that the crocodile was being gentle, and must admit Plumwood's survival had nothing to do with the crocodile reconsidering his behavior.

When describing the attack, as Plumwood did many times over the next years, she became aware of something confounding to any human. She remembers thinking: "This can't be happening to me, I'm a human being, I am more than just food!" She found it to be "a shocking reduction, from a complex human being to a mere piece of meat." She was in an "alien, incomprehensible world" in which, as she put it, the "narrative of self" had ended. She explains what she means by this phrase: she could not let go of herself entirely, and she wanted to tell her story. "During those incredible split seconds when the crocodile dragged me a second time from tree to water, I had a powerful vision of friends discussing my death with grief and puzzlement. The focus of my own regret was that they might think I had been taken while risking a swim. So important is the story and so deep the connection to others, carried through the narrative self, that it haunts even our final desperate moments."[3]

The more she reflected, the more her philosophy morphed into the notion that we humans are no different from any other species. *No* species wants to be prey to a predator. Each animal who is a victim is probably as shocked and horrified and terrified as she was. All animals, Plumwood saw, want to be more than prey.[4] Indeed, all animals *are* more than prey. "I was a vegetarian at the time of my encounter with the crocodile, and remain one today," she explained, and added: "This is not because I think predation itself is demonic and impure, but because I object to the reduction of animal lives in factory farming systems that treat them as living meat." She was responding to the insight that each and every animal has his or her own biography, an important point first made by the distinguished philosopher Tom Regan. This view is now accepted as one of the bedrock beliefs of people who work in the area of animal rights.[5] We have a tendency to believe that human biographies are more important than animal biographies, and it is worth noting that *every* animal has a past, and a desire to flourish and live a happy and full life.

I can remember riding a train out of Bombay when I was quite young and seeing the thousands and thousands of apartments with people crowded in them, and suddenly thinking: "They are just like me; they have their triumphs and their setbacks, just as I do. Although they are unknown to me and will always be unknown, their life matters as much to them as mine to me." Is this not equally true of every single animal on the planet?

Some Americans seem to believe that American lives are inherently more valuable than the lives of anyone Americans are at war with—for example, Afghans—so we often see reports, with minimal comment, of death by drone of entire families. For people who accept this degree of violence as normal, it is asking a lot to recognize that the lives of other animals are inherently valuable as well.

Alas, the crocodile *did* regard Valerie Plumwood as living meat. That is, after all, the major difference between humans and all other animal predators: we can make a choice about our diet that they cannot. She refused to allow the rangers to kill the crocodile who tried to kill her, as the animal had no real choice—it was simply doing what crocodiles must do to survive.

THE INTERNATIONAL UNION for the Conservation of Nature (IUCN) had listed the Nile crocodile as extinct in Mauritania in its 1992 action plan, but then in 1993 three young French travelers rediscovered them in five *gueltas* (rock pools). Today we know there are even more. Scientists from the University of Bonn in Germany conducted a study of *Crocodylus niloticus* in southeastern Mauritania.

The people in this area do not hunt the crocodiles—not for food nor for their skins. At least in the province of Hodh el Gharbi in southeastern Mauritania, the people believe that if they kill the crocodiles, their source of water will disappear and bad luck will descend permanently on their villages. Consequently, crocodiles are considered sacred, and harming them is taboo.

According to the German scientists, the children swim in the wetlands where the crocodiles live. The scientists saw women filling water containers with crocodiles basking in the sun right next to them. They also observed men making bricks next to a water hole filled with crocodiles, exhibiting no fear that at any moment they could be served up as lunch. Local farmers grow vegetables next to the *gueltas* inhabited by the crocodiles. Perhaps they lived with their losses? Not at all: there has not been a single report of any kind of attacks on humans in this area.

There are other traditional cultures where crocodiles are accorded this respect. The small African village of Paga in Ghana also has a tradition according to which the souls of ancestors are incarnated into crocodiles, and consequently the villagers do not harm the crocodiles in any way. There are more than a hundred crocodiles living in the lake beside the village, and nobody has ever been attacked by a crocodile, even though they bathe with them and interact with them as if they were playful pets.

Could it really be that, over time and with experience, crocodiles can learn to live in peace with the human species, much as the orca does? With thousands of years of cohabitation in the same ecological niche, have the crocodiles and the humans come to an understanding, a modus vivendi: "You leave us alone and we will leave you alone"? It is not entirely surprising that a species capable of compassionate behavior toward unrelated young (for this is true of crocodiles) might well decide that we are not to be harmed as long as we abide by the same code. Perhaps these crocodiles have myths about sacred humans, too, and believe that harming us will bring misery into their lives as well.

These are gentle crocodiles. How extraordinary! Coexisting with them, these people in Paga found a way to live in a world in balance. Does this prove that humans can learn to live in harmony with crocodiles, and if so, could that lesson be generalized? What would we look like as a species if we had greater respect for nature?

STILL, I MUST admit that when I visit Australia, if I am anywhere near where saltwater crocodiles or sharks might be found, I will not enter any body of water. The chances of being attacked may be infinitesimal, but I'm instinctively wary of these two apex predators.

But why the fear of alligators and crocodiles and sharks when the odds are so very much in our favor? Well, for one thing, becoming mortally wounded is no way to depart from this world. Crocodiles have the hardest known bite force on earth. Their jaw pressure is at least five times that of the largest lion. And whereas another alpha predator, the orca—the so-called killer whale—has never killed a human in the wild, crocodiles do, even if not often. Why the stark difference between these two species in terms of eating humans? Does it have to do with the fact that a crocodile has a much smaller brain than an orca? The disparity in brain size is a fact, but it is not necessarily relevant.

Crocodiles are more closely related to birds than they are to other reptiles. Crocodiles also live in complicated social environments, more similar to those of mammals than those of other reptiles. For example, a young crocodile who utters a distress call will attract immediate help from completely unrelated adult crocodiles, even if it means risking their lives. If we find this altruistic behavior surprising, it is merely an indication of how reluctant some humans are to recognize the intimate lives of this and other species.

Even so, crocodiles do kill people. Saltwater crocodiles are responsible for the death of approximately one person every year in Australia. The same is true, more or less, for alligators in North America (between 2000 and 2010, the American alligator killed thirteen people).

Like sharks, crocodiles do consume us. But, as I learned of villagers coexisting, even bathing, among crocodiles, I realized that it is not impossible to have a peaceable kingdom even with a species we consider innately murderous, if only people—and perhaps crocodiles, too—could agree to live and let live.

2 · "The Other"

It seems really very unfair that man should have chosen the gorilla to symbolize everything that is aggressive and violent, when that is one thing that gorillas are not, and that we are.

—Richard Attenborough

HUMANS SEEM TO HAVE A MANIA for hierarchy, which inevitably signals the wish to dominate another. In this hierarchy we judge someone or some other being to be inferior and hence ultimately dispensable. Extermination starts with finding differences. In searching for our species's singular capacity for violence, the first candidate for an explanation is our propensity to divide the world into "us" and "them."

Freud called it the narcissism of small differences. In *Group Psychology and the Analysis of the Ego*, elaborating on this human tendency, he writes one of the best accounts of it:

Every little canton looks down upon the others with contempt. Closely related races keep one another at arm's length; the South German cannot endure the North German, the Englishman casts every kind of aspersion upon the Scot, the Spaniard despises the

Portuguese. We are no longer astonished that greater differences should lead to an almost insuperable repugnance, such as the Gallic people feel for the German, the Aryan for the Semite, and the white races for the coloured . . . We do not know why such sensitiveness should have been directed to just these details of differentiation; but it is unmistakable that in this whole connection men give evidence of a readiness for hatred, an aggressiveness, the source of which is unknown, and to which one is tempted to ascribe an elementary character.[1]

While some ethnic distinctions may be invisible to us, for others they can be the cause of and justification for murder. For a long time many people around the world, for example, had hardly any awareness of ethnic differences in the former Yugoslavia: all who lived there were Yugoslavs. Yet ancient hatreds still simmered after hundreds of years.

In 1389, Serbian Christian knights faced an invading army of Ottoman Muslim Turks in Kosovo. Ottomans killed the Serbian leader, Stefan Lazar. This humiliation *more than six hundred years ago* has been offered as an explanation for the peculiar hatred that Serbs bear toward the Kosovars. As a result, to mark the six hundredth anniversary of the Battle of Kosovo, as it came to be known, the then-president of Serbia, Slobodan Milosevic, gave a speech in 1989 to cheering crowds, waving his picture next to that of Lazar. Milosevic delivered his speech on a huge stage with a backdrop containing powerful symbols of the Kosovo myth: images of peonies, a flower traditionally deemed to symbolize the blood of Lazar. We may well find this absurd or even comical, but the consequences were all too real and cost thousands of lives, culminating in the largest massacre of innocent civilians on European soil since the Second World War: at Srebrenica, Serbs murdered eight thousand men and boys after tying the victims' hands behind their backs. Lest we think this is something we find only in the Balkans, we can find versions of this in almost every country on earth and throughout history as well, at least after the advent of agriculture.

Fanning the flames of such deep-rooted hatred requires language, memory, and an almost inherited sense of grievance. We cannot imagine anything similar happening to any clan of animals: the mechanisms are not in place, nor is the stimulus. The puzzle may be why humans have allowed this to happen. Some blame our penchant for hierarchical order.

But don't wolves, too, have a rigid hierarchy, leading to the same kind of strife we find in human societies? Actually, wolves live in a family where the alpha female takes care of the pups (mind you, they are hers) while the alpha male is off on his travels foraging for food to bring back to the pack. Some of the other females are helping the female in her child care duties, while others accompany the hunters. Males, too, divide their activities: some will stay behind to help babysit; others join in the hunt. David Mech writes that in a natural wolf pack, "dominance contests with other wolves are rare, if they exist at all."[2] In the typical wolf pack, the alpha wolves are simply the breeding pair.

It would appear that wolves do not make the kinds of murderous distinctions that humans do. Wolves do not hunt down a wolf who has the wrong color. A wolf leader cannot order his pack into a pointless war against another wolfpack because he feels he has been insulted by another wolf. There are no murderous generals among wolves.

Yet many people think of wolves as vicious predators, willing to attack animals other than food prey. In fact, wolves are not like this at all. When forced into a dangerous encounter, they take the first opportunity to leave. That same response can be seen in dogs. Consider, for a moment, the implication of the descendants of wolves, namely dogs, behaving more humanely than humans.

Here is an extraordinary but little-known example: These days there are university departments of "alterity," the study of "otherness." They trace their lineage to the influential Lithuanian-born French philosopher and Holocaust survivor Emmanuel Levinas (1906–1995). "Otherness" played an important role in his philosophy: his last work, published the year of his death, was titled *Alterity and Transcendence*. He explains his discovery of alterity in autobiographical terms in a single paragraph that has captivated the imagination of many French philosophers.

While Levinas was in Freiburg in 1928, studying with Edmund Husserl, he met and was influenced by Martin Heidegger. In 1930, Levinas became a French citizen, and when war broke out, he was ordered to report for military duty. When the Germans invaded France in 1940, his unit was surrounded and quickly surrendered. He spent the rest of the war as a French prisoner of war in a camp near Hannover. He writes:

> About halfway through our long captivity, for a few short weeks, before the sentinels chased him away, a wandering dog entered our lives. One day he came to meet this rabble as we returned under guard from work. He survived in some wild patch in the region of the camp. But we called him Bobby, an exotic name, as one does with a cherished dog. He would appear at morning assembly and was waiting for us as we returned, jumping up and down and barking in delight. For him, there was no doubt that we were men. This dog was the last Kantian in Nazi Germany.

Karl Popper in *The Open Society and Its Enemies* summarized Kant's philosophy as: Always recognize that human individuals are ends, and do not use them as means to your end. For the dog, but not for the German soldiers, then, these men were simply men— not Jewish men, or prisoner men, just men.

Baboons, too, have strict dominance hierarchies, both for females and for males. While it is true that dominant males produce more offspring (and for many male baboons this could be said to be their very raison d'être), it is also true that females often choose *less* dominant, older, weaker males as their partners for reasons that are still somewhat obscure, possibly because they just like them. Moreover, more recent work on hierarchy in animal societies in general is tending to show that lower-ranking animals, especially males, may well live longer lives. Stress hormones in baboons and other animals at the top of the hierarchy are elevated, this research shows.[3] I am sure these same stress hormones would be found in Serbian soldiers ordered into genocidal battles, but our species has so institutionalized hierarchy that we don't make allowances for those who would rather just sit this one out.

Hierarchy in animals allows the elites to meet concrete needs: access to food and water, opportunities to mate, and so on. In humans, hierarchy seems to involve more than basic needs and to entail attempts to exalt ourselves at the expense of someone else. The "other" is deemed inferior, and we are not to feel any particular empathy or even sympathy for him. Hierarchy allows us to engage in genocide when no other animal does. Hierarchy is thus bad not just for individuals but for entire societies—indeed, one might say even for our entire species. That is why so many historians have attempted to pinpoint the moment in human history when hierarchy arose.

HUMANS HAVE FOUND it necessary to differentiate ourselves from animals in order to feel moral superiority. The use of nonhumans as insults is evident the moment we consider how many derogatory terms derive directly from names of animals. The list is almost endless, and such terms are to be found in most languages, certainly those I am most familiar with: French, German, Spanish, and English. Let me give just a small sample here, beginning of course with the word *animal* itself (*beast* and *brute* are not far behind): *ape, turkey, chicken, jackass, goose, cow, dog, pig, viper, rat, sheep, shrimp, skunk, shark, snake, toad*; then a whole class of animals, as when you call someone an *insect*—specifically a *leech, cockroach, louse,* or *worm.* When we say that somebody is a *bird-brain, batty, catty,* or a *predator,* our language shows our own ignorance and prejudice.[4]

Possibly the most persistent distinction humans make, right after the one between ourselves and other animals, revolves around religion. Religious loyalties are intimately connected to war, as many authors have noted. In the sense of religion being a specific ideology, we can claim that *all* wars are religious wars. We are fighting people who believe different things, worship different gods, and refuse to recognize that there can be only one true religion (mine) and that all others (yours, for example) are false. All beliefs that are not part of the one true religion are false beliefs. All behavior not dictated by that religion is heresy. Ideology is often mere window dressing to hide avarice for control and access to resources.

In the Crusades, which lasted for more than two hundred years, everyone who was not a Catholic was a pagan and a heretic. But the soldiers themselves were motivated in their notion of a "just" war. Popes and cardinals all over Europe both desired and strongly encouraged the spilling of blood in the name of Jesus. Eternal damnation awaited those who had committed sins, especially the sins of enemies. Only by dying in a holy war for Jerusalem could the faithful hope for remission, that is, forgiveness of sins, and entry into heaven. According to the Crusaders, it was God's wish that the Crusaders massacre Jews and Muslims.

Over the centuries that the Crusades operated, it may have been inevitable that violence would be extended not only to people of different religions but also to Christians who held different views. Thus Pope Eugene III and the Catholic Church initiated the Albigensian Crusade of the twelfth century to eliminate the Cathar heresy in Languedoc.[5]

The Cathars, the Church felt, were far too influenced by Gnosticism. Unusual for the Middle Ages, the Cathars condemned all violence, even the killing and eating of animals, and certainly going to war or engaging in capital punishment.

The Crusaders had no such restrictions on their violent tendencies. So the leader of the Crusaders, Simon de Montfort, ordered his troops to gouge out the eyes of a hundred prisoners, cut off their noses and lips, and then send the mutilated people back to the towers led by a prisoner with one remaining eye. When Arnaud-Amaury, abbot of Cîteaux, one of the commanders, was asked how to tell Cathars from Catholics, he replied, "Kill them all, the Lord will recognize His own."

This reply has inspired much imitation, in deed if not in word. The Crusaders broke down the doors of the Church of St. Mary Magdalene in the town of Béziers and dragged out and slaughtered the refugees, numbering seven thousand. They blinded, mutilated, and used for target practice many more of the townspeople. Arnaud wrote to Pope Innocent III, "Today, Your Holiness, twenty thousand heretics were put to the sword, regardless of rank, age, or sex." The Albigensian Crusade also had a role in the creation and institutionalization of both the Dominican Order and the medieval Inquisition. This is how the Crusades shaded into the Inquisition, and the same set of bad ideas operated at full throttle in both.

During the Spanish Inquisition, the worry was about conversos and Marranos—that is, Jews who, although they had converted to Christianity, were still suspected of secretly practicing Judaism. They were nothing but crypto-Jews after all, said the inquisitors. An element of paranoia underlies all attempts to uncover differences that are not readily apparent, the paranoia conspicuous by its absence in all other animal species. The name of the first Grand Inquisitor, the Dominican monk Tomás de Torquemada—who never traveled without a bodyguard of three hundred armed men—is practically synonymous with particularly cruel fanaticism. At least forty thousand Jews were forced to leave Spain as a result of Torquemada's influence over Ferdinand and Isabella, and up to two thousand were burned at the stake in public autos-da-fé. Evidence is mounting that Torquemada was probably of Jewish ancestry himself. He makes an appearance in one of the most famous set pieces in literature, Dostoevsky's *The Brothers Karamazov*, where he tells Christ, who has come back to earth in Seville at the time of the Inquisition, that he must not attempt to give humans choice, for they cannot bear it. One might argue that animals have no choice; they behave according to instinct. They don't make a rational choice about what they will eat or whom they will fight, for example. We do have choices, yet how have we so departed from our own best interests? The answer, though complex, will define whether we survive as a species. That is why it is so important to investigate the history of the mistakes of our species. Slavery is one such gigantic historical species-specific mistake.

THE CENTRAL ISSUE of the American Civil War, which cost nearly a million lives, was certainly slavery. Nearly four million people in the United States were enslaved when the war began in 1861, representing one third of the population of the South. The matter came to a head in 1857 with the Supreme Court decision in *Dred Scott v. Sandford*. Chief Justice Roger B. Taney's opinion said that slaves were "so far inferior that they had no rights which the white man was bound to respect." In other words, a slave was the ultimate "other" and was thus declared inferior, for inherent to the concept of slavery was the right to abuse anyone labeled as a slave.

Slavery is at the heart of any inquiry into the us/them distinction, and nothing has been more pernicious or more difficult to eradicate. The Texas Declaration of Causes for Secession said that the non-slave-holding states were "proclaiming the debasing doctrine of equality of all men, irrespective of race or color." The African race, the declaration continued, was "rightfully held and regarded as an inferior and dependent race." Slavery, so the South argued, was essential to its idea of manhood (presumably real men owned other men). In 2011, Americans marked the 150th anniversary of the start of the Civil War. Some of those celebrating the anniversary are still blind to the legacy of slavery, concentrating instead on the "genius" of certain Southern generals.

In every war, it is essential to let the soldiers on each side know that they are superior to those on the other side. Demeaning the enemy, denying him humanity, is essential and has probably been part of every war in human history.

How can it be so easy to convince one human of the *in*humanity of another?

3 · Conformity

Science may be the cumulative elimination of error, but the human fondness for toxic ideas is remarkably constant.

—John Gray

BY DEFINITION, THOSE WHO REFUSE TO go along with the majority are in the minority. Think of such whistle-blowers as Daniel Ellsberg, Jeffrey Wigand, Jesselyn Radack, Joseph Wilson, Wendell Potter, Chelsea Manning, Julian Assange, and Edward Snowden.[1] Most of these people held positions in government, industry, or the armed forces. Each discovered something seriously wrong and attempted to get that information out, first to the people who needed to know it and then to the general public. While they were heroes to some, the companies and organizations they worked for reviled them. All suffered persecution in one way or another, ranging from a court case that could have sent them to prison for the rest of their lives (Daniel Ellsberg, Chelsea Manning) to death threats (Jeffrey Wigand), subjecting a spouse to danger (Joseph Wilson and his wife, Valerie Plame), or the loss of a job (Jesselyn Radack, a former ethics adviser to the United States Department of Justice who complained of ethics violations by the FBI). There is no reward for these courageous individuals who simply told the truth.

Each and every one of them is slandered, often in the mainstream press. One example among many: the *Wall Street Journal* and the *Washington Post* called Joseph Wilson a liar. In reality, the willingness to engage in whistle-blowing—or, as I prefer to call it, telling the truth—ought to be the single most valuable character trait in anyone who works for a company, a university, or the government. It is the quality I hope my children will develop. "We are the truth-telling species" would be a wonderful thing to be able to say. But I have brought up whistle-blowing here to indicate how difficult it is in *any* human society to part company with the established wisdom.

The roots of this conformity to society go way back and are established early and deep. Our better writers are constantly finding new illustrations of that. Shirley Jackson's disturbing short story "The Lottery" describes a village of some three hundred people in what is clearly meant to be rural America, the heartland, which practices an ancient ritual every year in which one person wins the lottery. Throughout the story we are not sure what winning entails, though the atmosphere becomes increasingly disturbing, until four sentences from the end of the story we are told, "A stone hit her on the side of the head."

The story is about scapegoating as savagery, of how we feel inclined to simply go along with what has always been and encourage one another to do so, even when it involves a violent and unnecessary death. We learn not to question until we are the one selected. *The Visit* by the Swiss dramatist Friedrich Dürrenmatt also depicts a village easily corrupted into becoming murderers (in this case, by money).

Perhaps the single most popular example still remains Hans Christian Andersen's *The Emperor's New Clothes*. The story is based on a fourteenth-century Spanish collection of tales, *Libro de los ejemplos*, one of the earliest prose works in Castilian Spanish, which is itself taken from older sources in Greek and Arabic. (Scholars of fable literature claim it comes from an Indian text; I have not, however, been able to find the Sanskrit original of any similar story.)[2]

There was also a personal motivation in Andersen's case. In 1872 he recalled having stood in a crowd with his mother many years earlier waiting to see King Frederick VI of Denmark and Norway. When the king made his appearance, Andersen cried out, "Oh, he's nothing more than a human being!" His mother tried to silence him: "Have you gone mad, child?" The title of the story is now synonymous with any situation where an obvious truth is available only to a small child, who has somehow escaped the enculturation involved in defying our own senses.

IT IS NO secret that all human societies use the plasticity of childhood to instill their own values into the receptive mind of the child. We call it socialization or acculturation. It can be benevolent or not, depending on your position.

And yet the ability to agree, or at least be agreeable, is part of our species. Indeed, it is part of any species. Baby elephants grow up to be adult elephants in part by learning their place in the herd. All animals have a culture that they impart in one way or another to their young.[3] Yet it is clear that while a baby elephant learns what it means to be an elephant, she is not misled into believing, for example, that it is her duty to kill all animals who do not resemble elephants. Observation shows us that elephants, like all other herbivores, have as their dominant philosophy "Live and let live."[4] (Carnivores, of course, make an exception at dinnertime.)

I have always found British psychoanalyst Donald Winnicott's phrase "good-enough mothering"—referring to an "ordinarily devoted mother"—to be elusive, and I never understood why people find it so illuminating. (His notion of the "true" and "false" self is equally subjective.) On the other hand, a mother who manages to keep her child from becoming a carbon copy of herself in terms of beliefs and prejudices has indeed done a good job of mothering.

HERE, TOO, IS another simple but profound difference between us and other species: becoming an adult lion or tiger ten thousand years ago is hardly different than it is today. The requirements are the same. Same teaching, same methods, same goals. But bringing up a child today under the child-rearing standards of ten thousand years ago would result in disaster.

In most families, parents want their children to grow up to be like them: in attitudes, in values, perhaps even in profession (witness the many signs with some version of "Williams and Sons"). Don't lions and tigers expect their young to grow up to be like them? Sure, but our world changes every few years, whereas the world of lions does not or did not. So while human parents may well want their children to become like them, the child usually wants something else. Lions and other animals did not have that problem, at least until recently. Now, unfortunately, because we have encroached on the territory of just about every animal on earth, the chances of young lions, tigers, rhinos, and elephants *not* learning what it means to be an adult of their species increase exponentially. This is why just about any example of a wild animal behaving in a mysterious fashion, from elephant rape to honeybee colony collapse disorder, can be traced back to the trauma that humans create by interfering in the animals' normal habitat, the one that was a "good-enough habitat" (to coin a phrase) before we encroached and ruined everything, as we have a species-inherited tendency to do.

WHY IS IT, though, that we are socialized into racism, hatred, false views, and infinite ways to be cruel to others? Is this natural? Most other animals in the wild do not seem to be indoctrinated into actions that cause unnecessary misery to others. (Once again, I have to insist that when it comes to food we have a choice and they don't. So I do not consider the suffering that prey experience from a predator a form of cruelty.)

Orcas undergo nothing like human indoctrination. However, they do exhibit one behavior that causes concern. Is stranding— when whales beach themselves and cannot return to the ocean, sometimes singly, other times in mass strandings of entire whale pods—natural?[5] Isn't that something they learn to do that causes them untold grief? The question could be answered only if we knew the statistics for stranding hundreds of years ago, or perhaps even thousands of years ago, before humans interfered with whales.

The answer also depends on what we understand the reason for whale strandings in general to be. There is no one accepted explanation. Ingrid Visser, one of the leading authorities on orcas, suggests that orcas strand en masse because they do not want to leave their companions, and if one gets into trouble on dry land, stranded on the sand and unable to return to the ocean, the others come to his or her aid, often with fatal consequences.[6] Orcas did not grow up learning "If trouble comes, save yourself." On the contrary, they are taught that they must never abandon a sick or helpless or injured pod member. But if we believe that orcas strand because of increasing sonar noise, especially from large military ships in the ocean, something that causes their delicate sonar systems to jam, as it were, then we could say that circumstances alone create this problem. It is out of their control and is entirely the fault of humans.

There is increasing evidence that this is the case. In the year 2000, whales of four different species stranded themselves on beaches in the Bahamas. A government investigation revealed that a U.S. Navy battle group's use of sonar in the area was at fault. Bleeding in their ears was present often and is similar to decompression sickness. It is highly likely that sonar affects the whales' dive patterns with tragic results.

We, too, are subject to external trauma. Anthropologists use the term *environment of evolutionary adaptedness* (EEA) to refer to the "natural" conditions under which humans first evolved. The term comes from John Bowlby's book *Attachment and Loss*.[7] Bowlby was thinking of how babies need their mothers, the nourishment provided by the mother's breasts, and all the other natural needs of children as they grow up. Going to war was *not* part of our EEA.

It is important to know whether humans have *always* gone to war or whether this is something that has arisen at a specific time in the history of our species. I will save this discussion for later in the book, but I simply wish to point out that people's assumption that many human tendencies are inherent, or inborn, is really merely *one* point of view.

As an illustration, the distinguished Harvard professor of biology E. O. Wilson argued in his 1975 book, *Sociobiology*, that he and several other authors who study evolutionary biology, most notably Richard Alexander, consider among the 'noblest' traits of mankind such things as team play, altruism, patriotism, and bravery on the field of battle, which he considers to be the genetic product of warfare. I am not sure that Richard Alexander agrees with this summary, but I am sure that this is merely one point of view.

Perhaps nobody would argue with the value of altruism, but patriotism, on the other hand, is something that is very much in the eyes of the beholder. One person's patriotism is another person's nationalism. I don't think there is any universal agreement that it is a good thing. After all, there is no such thing in any hunter-gatherer society. Patriotism can, depending on your interpretation, be found either in the positive column of human traits or in the negative one.

Similarly, bravery on the field of battle is an interpretation of behavior we observe. We can never be certain whether that behavior is truly an example of altruistic bravery (which certainly exists) or merely hyperconformity, which also exists. As we know from recent research, most soldiers are reluctant to shoot and would take any opportunity to get out of harm's way.[8]

The resistance by soldiers to killing the enemy has been amply documented: in the Battle of Gettysburg in the U.S. Civil War, among soldiers from Argentina in the Falklands War, and among U.S. troops during World War Two (where it has been estimated that at most 25 percent of the combat soldiers shot at the enemy). General S. L. A. Marshall, who studied firing rates during World War Two, concluded, "The average and normally healthy individual ... [has] an inner ... resistance toward killing" (quoted by Lt. Col. Dave Grossman in *On Killing*).

It's highly questionable to call heroism or courage in battle desirable traits without further explanation or description of exactly what courage and heroism are. To go even further and claim these traits as genetic is even less likely to ensure universal agreement. It also forgets how much of human evolution is simply the product of "genetic drift," which refers to traits that are passed on purely by chance or as a result of a random process. That is part of evolution, yes, but it does not result in adaptations. Darwin wrote about how arms races begin: one person invents a more deadly weapon, his opponent must find an even nastier one, and so on.

If there is one insight I feel a reader should take away from this book, it is that *no serious evidence supports the idea that other animals besides humans engage in mass killing of one another.* The idea that they do is often found in popular books, even those written by scientists. So for example, Jared Diamond, in his *The Third Chimpanzee: The Evolution and Future of the Human Animal,* writes, "Accounts of murder and mass murder of animals by other animals of the same species are given by E. O. Wilson, *Sociobiology* (Cambridge, Mass.: Harvard University Press, 1975); Cynthia Moss, *Portraits in the Wild*, 2nd ed. (Chicago: University of Chicago Press, 1982); and Jane Goodall, *The Chimpanzees of Gombe* (Cambridge, Mass.: Harvard University Press, 1986)."[9]

I had read all those books and did not remember seeing anything about mass murder, so I looked again. The books Diamond cites do not give any examples of mass murder of animals by other animals of the same species. Even though these books, especially the one by Wilson, are comparatively old and one might have expected a less nuanced version of the evidence at that early time, I nonetheless failed to find any evidence of what Diamond alleges.

I could find nothing in Cynthia Moss's *Portraits in the Wild* on this topic. She is indeed one of the world's leading authorities on elephants, and it would be intriguing if she claimed they were capable of mass murder. She has, on the contrary, often spoken of how peaceable they are as a species. What she writes about lions, moreover, is quite the contrary of what Wilson claims: "Antagonistic encounters sometimes occur during competition over food, particularly if times are difficult, but for the most part the lions within a pride are amicable toward one another and there are few squabbles and fights. In fact, the impression a group of lions gives is one of lazy good fellowship." Mass murder?

On the other hand, Jane Goodall famously wrote: "The chimpanzee, as a result of a unique combination of strong affiliative bonds between adult males on the one hand and an unusually hostile and violently aggressive attitude toward nongroup individuals on the other, has clearly reached a stage where he stands at the very threshold of human achievement in destruction, cruelty, and planned intergroup conflict. If ever he develops the power of language—and, as we have seen, he stands close to that threshold, too—might he not push open the door and wage war with the best of us?"[10]

Chimpanzee attacks on members of their own group are explored in detail in chapter 5. The violence Goodall describes, disturbing as it is, does not rise to the level of mass murder. She concluded, in *Through a Window: My Thirty Years with the Chimpanzees of Gombe*, that what she saw among the chimpanzees was different from what she observes of our own species: "All around we see [human-caused] destruction and pollution, war and misery, maimed bodies, distorted minds, human and non-human alike." It was as if the chimpanzees developed the beginnings of greed, something unlikely to occur in the wild.

Goodall was the first to point out that chimpanzees have a "dark side to their nature." No longer could she see them as "rather nicer than human beings," as she once thought. But if there is another primate who resembles us in ugly ways, there are others who do not. Bonobos do not.[11] Most other primates—indeed, most other animals—do not, either.

According such importance to the aggressive side of chimpanzees without recognizing the other side seems to stack the deck. It feels as if we were doing something other than stating the facts as we find them. Richard Wrangham famously said in his influential book *Demonic Males: Apes and the Origins of Human Violence*, "Chimpanzee-like violence preceded and paved the way for human war, making modern humans the dazed survivors of a continuous, five-million-year habit of lethal aggression." This seems to me an overstatement, one that goes far beyond the evidence. Right-wing intellectuals such as Francis Fukuyama and Steven Pinker cite it with satisfaction.

Human nature is one of the slipperiest of all concepts. Is it part of our human nature to conform at all costs? What, then, are we to make of those who do not? It is more useful to realize that there is no such thing as a single human nature, and that this amazing diversity of behavior is an important part of what it means to be human.

This is what distinguishes us to some extent from most other species. For whereas elephants may diverge in their personalities, it is unusual to find an elephant who is completely different from all other elephants. How far out do you have to go in elephant society to be a true outlier? Pretty far. Not so for humans. If you look at statistics about basic beliefs in the United States, many people reading this book would be considered atypical or outliers.

For an elephant to be an elephant is to conform to elephant society. For humans, however, to be human can sometimes mean to struggle against what we have been taught to believe. Orwell knew that it was sometimes important to fight against the very beliefs one was raised with. Anything less has a tendency to lead to the worst forms of nationalism. "Us" versus "them" is not in our genes. It is something we learn.

4 · Cruelty

Of all the animals, man is the only one that is cruel. He is the only one that inflicts pain for the pleasure of doing it. It is a trait that is unknown to the higher animals.

—Mark Twain

IF WE DEFINE CRUELTY AS THE willful imposition of suffering when it is unnecessary, there are very few examples of cruelty in the wild. In a review of Roman Polanski's film *Carnage*, about how two apparently civilized New York couples can so easily be at each other's throats, a reviewer writes, "Beneath the surface of civilized behavior lurk animal impulses," but, in fact, animals do not behave this way. Child abuse is rampant in *all* human societies but absent in almost all animal societies (unless you consider infanticide to be that—a topic I will return to later). Violence against women, domestic violence, and stalking that is based in rejection—these are terms that can be applied only to human families. (In America, one in four women has been the victim of severe physical violence by an intimate partner.) Torture is completely absent from *all* animal societies, yet has been part of human history at least since agriculture arose ten thousand years ago, with hardly any diminution.[1] People often talk about torture in "antiquity," but what they are referring to is human societies (Scythians, Greeks, Romans, Persians, etc.) of the few centuries before the Christian era. As far as we know, there is no example of torture before the advent of warfare. Warfare, as the majority of scholars agree, began only about five thousand years ago, once we had agriculture. Before that, people simply walked away from conflict, as they owned nothing that required them to risk their lives protecting it. After they had fields and animals of their own and wanted to keep them from theft or appropriation, conflict between tribes increased exponentially, leading eventually to all-out warfare. Once you have war, you inevitably have torture.

I do not believe torture is natural in any sense of the word. Simply because it has been with us for the last ten thousand years does not mean it is part of our nature. The fact that it has a beginning in history shows that it is adventitious. I mean that it could almost be seen as accidental, and that we could, as a species, have gone in a different direction.

CONSIDER THIS QUOTE from chapter 35 of Dostoevsky's *The Brothers Karamazov*, in which Ivan is telling his brother Alyosha of the vicious nature of humans. Ivan gives accounts of unbearable cruelty to a child, and says:

> It's just their defenselessness that tempts the tormentor, just the angelic confidence of the child who has no refuge and no appeal, that sets his vile blood on fire. In every man, of course, a beast lies hidden—the beast of rage, the beast of lustful heat at the screams of the tortured victim, the beast of lawlessness let off the chain.

Dostoevsky is obviously aware of the immediate rejoinder, as Ivan continues: "People talk sometimes of bestial cruelty, but that's a great injustice and insult to the beasts; a beast can never be so cruel as a man, so artistically cruel." Dostoevsky raises an important question relevant more than a hundred years later: Why is it that a "beast can never be so cruel as a man"?

Whether acts of human kindness are rare or common does not undo the many acts of meanness and cruelty that we all are witness to on a daily basis, if only when reading the newspaper or getting on the Internet.

I DO NOT want to overstate my case, but I am suggesting that certain kinds of violence exist only in our species—namely, violence that has no evident purpose, which is how I define cruelty. When a male lion kills a young cub of a different father, the purpose (at an unconscious level) is to force the lioness into estrus so that *he* can father her next cub. We may not like infanticide in lions or other animals, but it has a clear evolutionary purpose. When human parents kill their children, on the other hand, it seems to be without evolutionary roots; it may sometimes be a result of what appears to be insanity, but most often it is an act of pure cruelty. Nor is it as rare as one might believe: homicide is the third-leading cause of death of American children five to fourteen years old.[2]

When we hunt animals we have no intention of eating, it is a kind of hunting very different from what we see in the wild, and it is done for recreation, not for need. Animals never go hunting for their own sake. To illustrate this point: bears don't hunt wolves, and wolves don't hunt bears. Researchers investigated 108 cases of wolf-bear interactions at feeding sites and wolf dens: "In 3 of the 108 cases, wolves killed bears, and in 2 others, vice versa; most such mortal interactions occurred at feeding sites."[3]

In other words, in 103 cases there was no killing. The bears and the wolves left each other alone. Neither is on the menu of the other, and even when they could kill one another, they do not do so. When humans hunt bears or wolves, it is an entirely different situation. We could argue that there was a time when we had no choice. That is not true today, and it is an example of how we have strayed from our better animal nature.

Humans find it hard to accept these facts, and so we invent scenarios that do not exist in reality. We claim lions and Cape buffalo (also called African buffalo) are natural enemies. We claim they hate each other. We also claim they don't like humans. We might be right about that. Never domesticated, these buffalo are among the most dangerous animals to humans in Africa, killing or goring some two hundred people every year. But then big-game hunters see Cape buffalo as trophy animals and hunt them for fun. Why shouldn't the animals object? They can run thirty-five miles an hour, but they will often suddenly stop running away and turn on a human pursuer, or even ambush him. But they never kill one another, ever.

We insist that the lions are cruel when they take down a buffalo calf. A YouTube video that has been seen by more than seventy-two million people, *Battle at Kruger*, shows a pride of five lions taking out a small calf. The herd of several hundred buffalo runs away and the lions begin the slow process of killing the calf. A crocodile tries to take the calf from the lions so he can eat the calf on his own. All the while, the calf is calling for help. The sound a calf makes in distress is rendered as *waaaaa* and is very similar to the crying of a human baby. The herd hears her distress calls, and suddenly all the animals stop. Then, to the viewers' surprise and delight, the entire herd turns around and heads back toward the struggling calf. Among the most gregarious animals in Africa, they obviously care deeply about their calves. The buffalo surround the lion pride and slowly approach the young calf. The giant cats snarl menacingly. The buffalo are not intimidated. They clearly mean business. Suddenly a big male buffalo (they can weigh up to two thousand pounds) charges one of the lions, gets him on his horns, and tosses him in the air. Emboldened, the others rout the lions and rescue the little guy, who appears none the worse for the mauling.

We humans cheer. But consider what the lions are doing: they are simply sitting down to a meal. *We* may well interpret this as cruel. But if we were to take the same calf and put him into our system of slaughterhouses, his fate would be no less cruel. Veal calves, no less adorable than this calf, are removed from their mother at birth and then slaughtered after several months of living in a small crate tethered to the front of the stall so that virtually all movement is restricted. Is this not torture?

I am confident lions do not intend to cause suffering when they take down their prey. They are designed in such a way that they *must* be predators to live. It is inconceivable that a lion would choose not to eat meat. But humans are a different type of predator, one with a conscience, for choice always means we can know what we are doing, even if we choose not to know or to ignore what we know in our hearts. We know we have such a choice because from early times there have been people who chose not to eat meat (at least since 1000 B.C.E., at the time of the Upanishads, and a few hundred years later, with the Greek philosopher Pythagoras).

As THE GREATEST predator in the ocean, similar to humans on land, orcas eat pretty much whatever they want. (The orca is known as the killer whale—no other animals in the ocean are able to escape should an orca decide to eat them.) Even the enormous sperm whales are at their mercy. But what they want is determined by orca culture. So there are orcas who eat primarily salmon; others eat only marine mammals; some specialize in other species of whales.[4] Watching the clip where the renowned David Attenborough walks us through a pod of killer whales targeting a gray whale and her newborn calf is a harrowing experience.[5] The mother gray whale does everything she possibly can to keep her calf from the killer whales. You can tell how frantic she is, and how terrified her young calf is. The orcas want the baby's tongue. It is hard to watch and even harder to think about. From our point of view they do not "need" to eat that tongue. Yet need I point out the obvious? Humans eat tongue as well, and there is only one way to get it. After all, when you come right down to it, there is only one food on the planet that is clearly meant to be eaten by humans, designed specifically for us, and that is breast milk. The rest of our diet is entirely cultural.[6] As for our horror at the thought of any animal killing for the sheer pleasure of it . . .

So what do we mean when we say that the orcas are being cruel by separating the mother from her calf and then ripping out the tongue of the baby and allowing her to slowly die from the loss of blood? The orcas did not eat the rest of the calf, only the tongue. We see this as cruel because we have distance from it. *We* are not hungry, nor are we orcas. It does not mean that orcas are not capable of compassion.

A ship belonging to the British Columbia Ferries fleet was on its way from Comox to Powell River in 1973 when it encountered orcas. The captain heard a crunch. Four killer whales surfaced a short distance away, and the captain noticed that one of the whales was bleeding profusely. The boat drew up to within ten feet of the whales to see what could be done. The captain described the scene:[7]

> The pod consisted of a bull, cow and two calves. It was one of the calves that had been struck by the ship's propellers. It was a very sad scene to see. The cow and the bull cradled the injured calf

between them to prevent it from turning upside-down. Occasionally the bull would lose its position and the calf would roll over on its side. When this occurred the slashes caused by our propeller were quite visible. The bull, when this happened, would make a tight circle, submerge, and rise slowly beside the calf; righting it, and then proceed with the diving and surfacing. While this was going on the other calf stayed right behind the injured one. We stayed with the whales for about ten to fifteen minutes; there was no fear of the ship being too close (about ten feet at times). I felt at the time that there was very little we could do to alleviate the obvious pain and suffering that was taking place and that the calf could not survive for too long. It appears that the young whale did live for at least fifteen days. We later received a report from a resident of Powell River, who, on 10 January 1974, observed "two whales supporting a third one, preventing it from turning over." We do not know whether the whale survived after this, as we received no further sightings or photographs from which we could identify the individual.

Clearly, orcas (*Orcinus orca*) do not deserve to be called killer whales. The orca is a member of the peaceable dolphin family, the largest member of that family. They are found in all oceans of the world. They are impressive animals to see: the males are as large as thirty-two feet and can weigh up to eighteen thousand pounds, and on average an orca eats five hundred pounds of food a day. So these are very big animals, which no doubt leads us to see them as aggressive. Why size should correlate with aggression in the human mind is not clear, but it does, in spite of the facts.

In many ways, orcas resemble humans. They protect and care for injured and sick individuals. Females become sexually mature between ten and eighteen years of age. They live about as long as do humans. Like us, they have no natural enemies. Next to humans, they are the most widely distributed of all mammals, found in every ocean of the world. Young calves nurse for at least a year, and possibly longer. We know quite a lot about the culture of different groups of orcas: "The complex and stable vocal and behavioural cultures of sympatric [closely related] groups of killer whales appear to have no parallel outside humans and represent an independent evolution of cultural faculties."[8] In other words, they learn and they pass on what they learn. Each pod has its own traditions—how they communicate, what they eat, and what kind of behavior they display. Some pods are gentle, others more macho, entirely due to the culture they grow up in.

You would think that this extraordinary similarity to humans, paralleled by no other animal in nature, would lead us to value them as an independent, almost human-like tribe—sovereign nations, if you like. We didn't know this in the past, so we simply killed them. Once we learned how similar they were to us, though, we realized they could be trained to perform for us, and now we capture them to entertain us. Orcas are, as the phrase goes, "dying" to entertain us.

Like us, orcas evolved to show compassion to their own, and not to members of another species. While it is true that orcas do not target humans, they can target just about any other mammal in their territory should they feel like it. Perhaps humans have not been seen as a prey species for whales because we came on the scene far too recently to have figured in their dietary habits. Orcas can, and do, eat other marine mammals, many of which we consider "cute," and which most of us don't eat (although the Inuit certainly did). The orcas have the brainpower to recognize the suffering they cause. They have tremendous emotional depth when it comes to the suffering of other orcas. So I am sure they understand what they are doing as well as we can when we slaughter lambs.

An orca's brain is nearly four times the size of a human brain, which does not mean that orcas are four times as intelligent, but it does indicate complexity. Both human and orca brains contain deep folds, especially in the frontal cortex, which are the hallmark of high social intelligence. The brain researcher Toni Frohoff has examined the orca brain and found that it is uniquely developed in a manner that enables the species to experience emotion to the same degree as humans, if not to a greater degree.

A detailed examination by Lori Marino, using MRI scanning, comes to a more cautious conclusion.[9] With respect to whale brains, in the last few years there have been major discoveries, mainly from the Mt. Sinai School of Medicine in New York. Orcas and some other dolphins and whales have been found to have spindle cells, which make possible deeper emotions and social bonds; previously these had been seen only in humans and some great apes. Humans are able to love and to suffer, it was thought, because we had these cells. Spindle cells, it was said, are the very cells that make us human. Now it turns out that whales have had these cells at least twice as long as we have (whales emerged as a species thirty million years ago), and they could have as many as three times the number that are found in the human brain. This would be one explanation for why whale brains are larger than human brains. It is not just that whales are bigger animals; they may have equally complex emotions, including a highly sophisticated intelligence. Clearly, however, they use that intelligence for purposes other than waging war: complex communications via song, for example.

Why is it our culture to kill members of our species? One might claim that this is part and parcel of our very nature; it defines what it means to be human. We have *always* been like that. Evolutionary biologists make this point frequently, if not completely convincingly. Edmund Burke, in his *A Philosophical Enquiry into the Origin of Our Ideas of the Sublime and Beautiful*, wrote, "I am convinced we have a degree of delight, and that no small one, in the real misfortunes and pains of others."

I am inclined to believe, however, that we have not always been like this. Here I join many anthropologists and paleoarchaeologists, as well as paleopathologists (people who study diseases in early humans). Jared Diamond popularized the thesis in a widely read article, "The Worst Mistake in the History of the Human Race."[10] In brief, he said that several recent discoveries (not his own) suggest that the adoption of agriculture, which many have thought of as a most decisive step toward a better life, was in many ways a catastrophe from which the human species has never quite recovered. This is because along with the advent of agriculture came social inequality, sexual inequality, and diseases unknown before, as well as the despotism of cruel leaders, a concept absent from earlier human societies.

Agriculture, which arose only between fifteen thousand and ten thousand years ago, represents only a very small fraction of our evolutionary history. For the vast majority of our past, humans were hunting (even if we hunted very little) and foraging or gathering (most of the time).[11] Anthropologists have pointed out that our health was better then, for we did not depend on any one crop: hunter-gatherers could have access to more than a hundred edible plants and herbs rich in nutrients. Contrary to popular opinion, we were even taller before agriculture: men were on average five feet nine inches and women five feet five inches in Turkey some twenty thousand years ago; thousands of years later, in 3000 B.C.E., humans were smaller, with men on average five feet three inches and women five feet. Again, contrary to common wisdom, we did not live longer lives once we had agriculture. George Armelagos points out, "Life expectancy at birth in the pre-agricultural community was about twenty-six years, but in the post-agricultural community it was nineteen years ... episodes of nutritional stress and infectious disease were seriously affecting their ability to survive."

Because there were no possessions (no fields, no crops) there was little to steal, and no class distinctions, no kings or venture capitalists to exploit the labor of others. Equality was necessarily the default societal position. Women were equal to men, since they found in the forest much of the food we ate. (As far as we can tell, men and women foraged equally.) Diamond's conclusion: "Hunter-gatherers practiced the most successful and longest-lasting life style in human history. In contrast, we're still struggling with the mess into which agriculture has tumbled us, and it's unclear whether we can solve it."

What Diamond doesn't comment on, however, is the other important factor: the domestication of plants was accompanied by the domestication of animals. They happened more or less simultaneously. Except for dogs, who were domesticated much earlier, the earliest animals to be domesticated were sheep, goats, pigs, and cows (from around 9000 B.C.E.).[12]

Obviously, the original point of animal domestication had to do with food. And of course, to eat animals, humans had to exclude the recognition that they had feelings and could suffer in much the same way we do. F. E. Zeuner, the greatest scholar of domestication, says, "The chief purpose of pig-breeding is undoubtedly that it is the most prolific and abundant supplier of meat and fat for the kitchen." Of course this is why pigs are bred, but it ignores the living animal, which can never be entirely a manufactured product, like a metal bucket.

So I would add to Diamond's list of the disadvantages of agriculture that the domestication of animals gave early humans far too much room to exercise cruelty. When we were hunter-gatherers, we simply killed an animal. There was no additional cruelty involved beyond that of the killing itself. It was hard enough to catch an animal. But when animals were kept penned, corralled, and fenced—in other words, when they were no longer free beings, the hunting of whom could be dangerous to humans—it made it easier for humans to ignore the true nature of the animal. I am sure there are many people who do not wish to be cruel but who nonetheless eat meat. But domestication of animals fed our worst instincts, or perhaps even created them in the first place.

People in early indigenous cultures (Inuit, Aboriginal, Amerindian, Maori, and so on) asked forgiveness of an animal before they hunted it down and killed it. When you compare this practice—which recognizes the seriousness of the act, and also the necessity and the reluctance with which a life was taken—with what happens today in any slaughterhouse, I can see how this earlier version of killing was more "civilized." The attempt to avoid cruelty, to teach young hunters precisely *not* to engage in cruelty, stemmed from the awareness of just how serious it was to take the life of another being. Killing may have been necessary, but it was not casual.

Surely cruelty existed before this opportunity to demonstrate it arose. Yet the psychology of cruelty does suggest that when there are occasions when it can be indulged in safely, secretly, or even sanctioned by society, it can spread dangerously and can even run amok.

Nobody in his right mind would ever want to fight a bull in the wild. It was domestication that suggested the use of bulls in bull-fighting, one that almost everyone now agrees is a prime example of human cruelty to animals. Speculating on the origins of human cruelty is valuable because it allows the possibility of reversal.

ARE APEX PREDATORS crueler than other animals? Animals who are *not* predators do not, by definition, eat other animals, but do they kill them? Usually they do not bother other weaker animals, let alone kill them. On the other hand, humans have not fared well with some vegetarian animals who are big and can be dangerous. Hippos, for example, while vegetarian, kill more humans in Africa than any other animal except, of course, the human animal. However, it is usually not the case that the humans are simply minding their own business and are targeted by a hippo out of innate ill will. Usually there is a reason for the attack, such as humans invading their territory, getting too close to hippo young, or even trying to kill them. Hippos are not dangerous to other animals in Africa.

David Phillips, an expert on whales, wrote to me saying,

Natural selection has honed the carnivores for aggressive predation. They have instinctual search images for their prey. It's built in. Food is survival and the top predators have to be efficient killers. The grazers have no such need. So, yes, the carnivores are primed for aggression; it's both in their genes and in their learned behaviors. That's why the occasional mistake by orcas with wetsuited surfers. They fit the search image and it triggers an automatic reaction by the orcas. However, they are so damn smart that the second they detect neoprene instead of sealskin I'm sure their reaction is "oops" and they quickly move on.

If this is so, and it makes sense, where do humans fit into this scheme? As a top predator, do we have to be efficient killers? There does seem to be some truth to the human habituation to cruelty. Children who torture pets are more likely to grow up to harm other humans. According to a 1997 study done by the Massachusetts Society for the Prevention of Cruelty to Animals and Northeastern University, animal abusers are five times more likely to commit violent crimes against people and four times more likely to commit property crimes than are individuals without a history of animal abuse. Ted Bundy, Jeffrey Dahmer, and other serial killers had a history of torturing animals. Eric Harris and Dylan Klebold, who shot and killed twelve classmates at

Columbine High School, bragged to their friends about mutilating animals.[13]

I had always hoped that people who are, on the contrary, particularly kind to animals, who would never hurt them (even, say, by eating them), are *less* likely than others to engage in human cruelty, especially of the kind that we associate with war. But just as human cruelty to animals may not eventuate in cruelty to other humans, so also a benign history toward animals is no guarantee of an equally benign history when it comes to humans. Nazi Germany was opposed to vivisection. Hitler's love of his German shepherd Blondi comes to mind as well. Mussolini, too, was fond of dogs and even turtles.

5 · War

The story of the human race is War. Except for brief and precarious interludes, there has never been peace in the world; and before history began, murderous strife was universal and unending.

—Winston Churchill

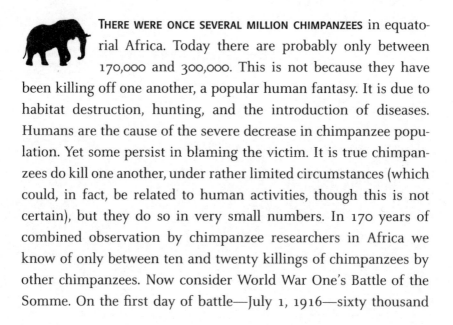THERE WERE ONCE SEVERAL MILLION CHIMPANZEES in equatorial Africa. Today there are probably only between 170,000 and 300,000. This is not because they have been killing off one another, a popular human fantasy. It is due to habitat destruction, hunting, and the introduction of diseases. Humans are the cause of the severe decrease in chimpanzee population. Yet some persist in blaming the victim. It is true chimpanzees do kill one another, under rather limited circumstances (which could, in fact, be related to human activities, though this is not certain), but they do so in very small numbers. In 170 years of combined observation by chimpanzee researchers in Africa we know of only between ten and twenty killings of chimpanzees by other chimpanzees. Now consider World War One's Battle of the Somme. On the first day of battle—July 1, 1916—sixty thousand

British soldiers were killed or gravely wounded, thirty thousand of these in the first half hour. At the end of four and a half months of battle, both sides had sustained 1.3 million casualties, and the British and French front line had advanced five miles.

Warfare and genocide are unique to humans. However, it is not only warfare and genocide but also the notion of murdering fellow humans—even those who belong to the same clan, tribe, or nation—that takes much of human behavior out of the animal realm altogether.

How many of his fellow Russians did Stalin kill? Robert Conquest, in his classic 1968 book *The Great Terror: Stalin's Purge of the Thirties*, reviews a number of estimates and calculates that the number of executions from 1936 to 1938 was probably about 1 million; from 1936 to 1950 about 12 million died in the camps, and 3.5 million died in the 1930–36 collectivization. Overall, he concludes, we get a figure of 20 million dead. This is the figure generally used, but Conquest goes on to say that this figure "is almost certainly too low, and might require an increase of 50 percent or so." The high end is the 60 million suggested by Alexander Solzhenitsyn.

By 1938, Conquest estimates, about 7 million purge victims were in the labor/death camps, on top of the hundreds of thousands who had been slaughtered outright. In the worst camps, such as those of the Kolyma gold-mining region in the Arctic, the survival rate was just 2 or 3 percent. Solzhenitsyn calls the prison colonies in the Solovetsky Islands "the Arctic Auschwitz," and cites the edict of their commander, Naftaly Frenkel, which "became the supreme law of the Archipelago: 'We have to squeeze everything out of a prisoner in the first three months—after that we don't need him anymore.'"[1]

According to the declassified Soviet archives, during 1937 and 1938 the NKVD (secret police) detained 1,548,366 victims, of whom 681,692 were shot—an average of 1,000 executions a day.

It is hard to know what to call this mass killing of people for no discernible reason, beyond paranoia and sheer human cruelty. I think we are justified in calling Order No. 00447 of 1937 genocide. It called for the mass execution and exile of "socially harmful elements" as "enemies of the people." In the process of collectivization, for example, thirty thousand kulaks (wealthy peasants, or rather, peasants wealthier than other peasants) were killed directly, mostly shot on the spot. About two million were forcibly deported to the Far North and Siberia. These people were called not only "enemies of the people" but also "swine," "dogs," "vermin," "half animals," and "apes."

Stalin and Lenin did not kill tens of millions of people without the collaboration of hundreds of thousands of other people. In fact, we know that as soon as the 1937 kulak operation was launched, regional party and NKVD bosses—eager to show their zeal and their loyalty to the party, and especially to Stalin himself—demanded and got an increase in the quotas. Probably they were also afraid they could be next, fear feeding cruelty.

It is difficult to imagine the suffering during this time. The most affecting account I have read is Alexander Solzhenitsyn's searing three-volume work, *The Gulag Archipelago*, based on his own prison experience and that of 256 other former prisoners. One comes away from the book with a sense that you have understood something of human nature that you would rather not have known.

The only way to convey the horror of this time is to quote from direct testimony. Vsevolod Meyerhold was a Russian theater director arrested in 1939 and shot in 1940. (In 1955 he was posthumously cleared of all charges.) He wrote in a letter sent from prison just before he was shot:

The investigators began to use force on me, a sick 65-year-old man. I was made to lie face down and beaten on the soles of my feet and my spine with a rubber strap . . . For the next few days, when those parts of my legs were covered with extensive internal hemorrhaging, they again beat the red-blue-and-yellow bruises with the strap and the pain was so intense that it felt as if boiling water was being poured on these sensitive areas. I howled and wept from the pain. I incriminated myself in the hope that by telling them lies I could end the ordeal.

Stalin not only acted in cold blood but was deceitful in ways that seem almost incomprehensible: Two of his comrades whom he had arrested, Grigory Zinoviev, head of the Communist International, and Lev Kamenev, premier in the last year of Lenin's life, demanded, as a condition for "confessing," a guarantee from the Politburo that their lives and those of their families would be spared. At a private meeting, Stalin gave them such assurances. After the trial, Stalin not only broke his promise to spare the defendants but also had most of their relatives arrested and shot.

Anyone and everyone could be accused and killed. Even Jan Sten, a philosopher and deputy head of the Marx-Engels Institute, in spite of having been Stalin's private tutor, was seized on the direct order of Stalin and put to death. Others well known in the West include the poet Osip Mandelstam and the writer Isaac Babel. The author of *Dr. Zhivago*, Boris Pasternak, barely escaped murder. In Mongolia, Buddhist priests made up the majority of victims, with eighteen thousand killed. Even the army was not excluded: about thirty-five thousand military officers were shot or imprisoned. The destruction of the officer corps, and in particular the execution of the brilliant chief of staff Marshal Tukhachevsky, is considered one of the major reasons for the spectacular Nazi successes in the early months of the German invasion of the Soviet Union in 1941. The Soviets lost their most valuable and experienced officer at a time when they could least afford to do so.

Stalin certainly knew that most if not all the people he had murdered were innocent of any of the charges. Perhaps he believed, like Lenin, that it was necessary to victimize many innocents if all of the guilty were to be apprehended. Or did he even truly believe anyone at all was guilty of the trumped-up charges? The idea of enemies lurking everywhere is basic not just to dictators but to entire countries. Indeed, one could say it characterizes our species. The insanity of all those horrors simply boggles the mind. "What is it with us?" we can't help wondering over and over as we read about such events, and even more so should we have the misfortune to actually have experienced them.

Raymond Chandler in his novel *The Long Goodbye* summed up the human condition pretty well: "Twenty four hours a day somebody is running, somebody else is trying to catch him. Out there in the night of a thousand crimes, people were dying, being maimed, cut by flying glass, crushed against steering wheels or under heavy tires. People were being beaten, robbed, strangled, raped, and murdered." Or more succinctly, in Kurtz's last words summing up what the colonial powers did in Africa, in Joseph Conrad's *Heart of Darkness*: "The horror! The horror!" Philip Larkin's unforgettable poetic lines also come to mind: "Man hands on misery to man. It deepens like a coastal shelf."

We are so accustomed to taking the word of evolutionary biologists about the roots of humanity's more awful traits that we don't question how relevant the source really is. Thus when we are assured that rape occurs in many other animals, we nod in understanding and commiseration, adding, "I guess we are just like other animals after all." But other animals rarely rape, and when they do, it has to do with reproduction, not random viciousness. The males unconsciously "want" their genes to proliferate. They want offspring. They are not interested in hurting females.

That's very different from human rape. During the Spanish Civil

War, the African militias fighting on the side of Franco routinely raped girls after conquering a city. This was considered an important part of psychological warfare, done to break down any remaining resistance. "The legionaries showed the Red cowards and their women what it means to be a man. This is justified because these anarchists and communists advocated free love," said Gonzalo Queipo de Llano, one of Franco's infamous generals.

Animals are indeed different. As the distinguished animal scientist Pat Shipman told me, "I have not found any report of forced sex with juveniles in nonhuman primates. Although bonobos are reported to engage in frequent sex in 'all possible combinations'—including adults with juveniles—they do not have sex with unwilling partners."[2]

Child sexual abuse is often about violence, even murder. The first example that Freud saw of child sexual abuse at the Paris morgue involved the autopsy of a child who had been raped and murdered by her father. I am unaware of any similar behavior in any animal species.

MANY OF OUR notions of how animals fight to the death for status or other privileges are often little more than misinformation. For example, the bad temper of many camels is legendary, and it has been claimed that during the rutting seasons, males, even if neutered, will sometimes fight to the death. But Hilde Gauthier-Pilters, who observed camels for years in the Western Sahara among the Reguibat, the only remaining pure nomads, saw just one serious fight between two males, and neither animal was killed.

Giraffes almost never fight, either among themselves or with other species, and in any outdoor enclosure you are likely to see giraffes with zebras, wildebeest, ostriches, elands, baboons, and various other animals, living amicably together. There are no records of a giraffe harming *any* animal except in self-defense. The only form of combat is a ritualized one of necking, where two males wrap their necks around each other in an attempt to determine mating priority, but this has rarely been seen to eventuate in harm.

Strict vegans, giraffes are able to browse where other animals cannot go, allowing them freedom from any sense of territoriality. They have a natural curiosity and are friendly even with their single greatest enemy, humans. We kill them for their meat, for their hair, and for their skin to make bracelets, rope, and guitar strings. There are probably only 80,000 left in all of Africa, whereas in 1999 the total number of giraffes in Africa was estimated by the IUCN to exceed 140,000. This is a considerable drop in a single decade. I find it sad to think that my grandchildren may ask: "What is a giraffe?"

There is aggression among animals, of course, but it is rarely deadly. Moreover, all animal violence, without exception, obeys certain rules. For example, chimpanzees and wolves do not like to have their territory invaded by members of a different troupe or pack. On rare occasions, they will defend their territories with fights unto death. There are struggles for access to food and for access to mates. Even then, the intent does not seem to be to kill. That's the equivalent of involuntary manslaughter, rather than murder in the first or second degree.

WHENEVER SOMEBODY LIKE me tries to claim that humans are a uniquely violent species, the question of warfare among chimpanzees is raised. (Consider how many movies there are in which the chimps are the warmongering soldiers.) Strictly speaking, chimpanzees are not predators. Most of their nourishment comes from plant foods, and only a small proportion (5 percent) from animal protein. On the other hand, the popular imagination is saturated with the idea that chimps engage in warfare and murder, and in that they are like us, and since we share some 99 percent of our genes with them, this explains human violence.

It is true that we are close genetically to chimpanzees, but we are still two completely different species. Dogs and wolves, on the other hand, are genetically almost identical, so much so that one could not identify which is dog and which is wolf from DNA alone. Yet their behavior when it comes to aggression is completely different. The reasons are cultural (or historical, if you like). Not only are dogs and wolves different from each other, but each dog is different from every other dog, and so is every wolf (but perhaps not to the extent that dogs are, undoubtedly because of our influence on dogs).[3] So, of course, are humans. When we attempt to understand one person's murderous behavior, we tend to look at that person's life, not at the species. We don't dismiss a murderer by saying: "Well, that's what men are like. They were like that in prehistory and they are still like that." Of course, not all men—or even most men—are like that, even if some are. In the past as well, some were murderers and some were not. Can we not say the same of chimpanzees?

Chimpanzees, gorillas, and bonobos are closely related to one another genetically, yet the three differ completely in their behavior. Gorillas and bonobos are, by and large, peaceful; they also are primarily vegetarian. Bonobos practice a form of Gandhian nonviolence. The females form coalitions and are able to "take back the night" from any male foolish enough to entertain violent thoughts against them.

The idea of war among the chimps first surfaced because of what Jane Goodall had seen in Tanzania's Gombe National Park, known locally as Kasekela. Initially in the 1960s and into the early 1970s, Goodall saw the benign side of these animals. She was the first to recognize how much like us chimpanzees were in their feelings. She described, memorably, how one chimpanzee in particular, whom she called David Greybeard, opened a door for her into the mind and feelings of chimpanzees, a major break-through at the time:

> I had been following David one day, struggling through dense undergrowth near a stream. I was thankful when he stopped to rest, and I sat near him. Close by I noticed the fallen red fruit of an oil nut palm, a favorite food of chimpanzees. I picked it up and held it out to David on the palm of my hand. For a moment I thought he would ignore my gesture. But then he took the nut, let it fall to the ground and, with the same movement, very gently closed his fingers around my hand. He glanced at my face, let go of my hand, and turned away. I understood the message: "I don't want the nut, but it was nice of you to offer it." . . . It was a moment of revelation. I wanted to be alone, to ponder the signifi-cance of what had happened, to enshrine those moments perma-nently in my mind.[4]

That moment was the beginning of the modern knowledge of the mind and emotions of one of our closest animal relatives.

Slowly, though, the original chimpanzees whom Goodall thought she knew so well began to form two distinct communities. One could almost call them tribes. The primatologist Richard Wrangham, who as a graduate student in the early 1970s went to work as a research assistant to Goodall, began to notice what looked like gang behavior; tough males defending their territory, "committed," as he put it, to "ethnic purity." Goodall too noticed a violent change. It shocked her deeply.

It wasn't just that the animals were defending their territory, or patrolling their borders. They did this, too, but now they seemed far more agitated, as if they had undergone a complete change of heart, and they engaged in full-fledged raids. The purpose of the raids, so Wrangham observed, was to eliminate the other tribe one by one, killing them in horrible and gruesome ways. The same animals who had played together as youngsters and adolescents were now sworn enemies. The same animals who had been generous, fun, friendly, and kind to one another, laughing, taking care of the sick, were now capable of tearing one another from limb to limb.[5] Goodall later described the horrors she had seen:

> Fights on members of other communities are brutal in the extreme, often involving several (up to six has been seen) males against one victim. These gang attacks usually last for at least ten minutes, and they typically result in very severe wounding. During "the four year war" five savage assaults were actually observed; and we should remember that this brutality was directed against individuals who had previously been part of the same community. The victims of these attacks—which lasted up to twenty minutes—all died as a result of the terrible injuries they received. By the end of the four years the entire Kaham Community had been annihilated.[6]

There was even worse to come: "The four years from early 1974, when Godi was attacked, until late 1977, when Sniff was killed, were the darkest years in Gombe's history. Not only was an entire community annihilated but, in addition, there were the cannibalistic attacks of Passion and Pom, the gruesome feasting on the flesh of newborn babies."[7] Was this deliberate cruelty? No, insists Goodall: "Chimpanzees, it is true, are able to empathize, to understand at least to some extent the wants and needs of their companions. But only humans, I believe, are capable of *deliberate* cruelty— acting with the intention of causing pain and suffering."

What fundamental change had taken place among the

chimpanzees after fourteen years? Of course it is possible that such murderous rage and violence had occurred earlier but was concealed or somehow missed. But that was unlikely. Goodall began to question whether her decision in 1965 to start feeding bananas to the chimps might have played a role in their aberrant behavior:

> The constant feeding was having a marked effect on the behavior of the chimps. They were beginning to move about in large groups more often than they had ever done in the old days. They were sleeping near camp and arriving in noisy hordes early in the morning. Worst of all, the adult males were becomingly increasingly aggressive. When we first offered the chimps bananas, the males seldom fought over the food ... [now] not only was there a great deal more fighting than ever before, but many of the chimps were hanging around camp for hours and hours ever day.[8]

Goodall concedes: "When we first offered the chimps bananas the males seldom fought over their food; now there was a great deal more fighting than ever before."

This was an unplanned experiment on her part; Goodall did not expect it to lead to something we can almost recognize as war. What happened to the chimps is not unlike what happened to humans when agriculture was introduced into our hunter-gatherer way of life, which in many ways was identical to the lives of free-living chimpanzees.

But if chimpanzees in other sites were also killing, as Wrangham and others claim, then perhaps what Goodall had seen earlier, namely, a fairly peaceable species, was the exception, and violence the norm. It is not entirely clear what Goodall thinks now. She has written, "It is easy to get the impression that chimpanzees are more aggressive than they really are. In actuality, peaceful interactions are far more frequent than aggressive ones; mild threatening gestures are more common than vigorous ones; threats per se occur much more often than fights; and serious, wounding fights are very rare compared to brief, relatively mild ones."[9] We could say the same of humans, too, but it avoids the issue: is deliberate killing part of their nature, or is it something brought about by circumstances?

Goodall has gone on record as saying she believes that "once we accept that a living creature has feelings and suffers pain, if we knowingly and deliberately inflict suffering on that creature, we are equally guilty. Whether it be human or animal, we brutalize ourselves." When Bill Moyers told her in 2009, "But you learned from the chimpanzees that animals can be cruel, too," she answered, "Yes, but I think a chimpanzee doesn't have the intellectual ability, or I don't think it does, to deliberately inflict pain. You know, we can plan a torture, whether it's physical or mental. We plan it. And in cold blood we can execute it. The chimpanzee's brutality is always—you know, the spur of the moment. It's some trigger in the environment that causes this craze, almost, of violence."

Scholars are divided as to whether what Goodall saw was typical or aberrant. The evidence is unclear. Wrangham cites the work of Toshisada Nishida, who has been studying chimpanzees in Tanzania's Mahale Mountains National Park since 1965. From 1969 to 1982, seven males of one community disappeared one by one, until the community was extinguished. Nishida and his team think that some, maybe most of those who disappeared, were killed by neighbor chimps. But there is no direct evidence. Most primatologists believe, along with Richard Wrangham, that there is mounting evidence of deliberate killings in groups of chimpanzees in widely dispersed locations, even where there is no feeding by humans.[10]

Stanford University social psychologist Robert Zajonc points out that it would be "stretching the imagination" to equate what happens with chimpanzees to the vast murders of innocent civilians that routinely happens in human societies.[11] There is nothing like the level of atrocity in any animal species, he points out. Animal violence, he notes, is spontaneous and arises when there are disputes over access to resources. The threat is clear, and the opponent always has the choice of leaving. Zajonc says it well: "To assume that these cataclysmic events belong to a common category with the beating that eight chimpanzees inflicted on one of theirs nears on obscenity. The term *bestiality* when characterizing human violence is an offense to the nonhuman species."

Wrangham and others believe raids and murder are an integral part of chimpanzee nature. And this, for Wrangham, holds lessons for humans: "Our warring tendencies," he wrote, "go back into our prehuman past." He notes that most animals are nowhere near as violent as humans, and wonders why deadly violence evolved in humans. Why not drive the enemy away, as animals do, rather than kill him? The only animal who behaves anything like this are chimpanzees and ourselves. "Perhaps," Wrangham speculates, "only chimpanzees and humans have enough brainpower to realize the advantages of removing the opposition." This is an uncharitable view of intelligence, one that allows us to slaughter our enemies, whereas less intelligent animals only wish to scare them away!

But to believe this has had selective advantages for humans, you have to agree with Wrangham's view that "the tough guy finds himself besieged with female admirers, while the self-effacing friend sadly clutches his glass of Chablis at the fern bar alone." But this view of male machismo has been relegated to the large pile of silly ideas that justify chauvinism as "just the way things are." In real life, most women do not prefer men who fight one another in bars.

Wrangham's book *Demonic Males* does not argue that humans are inevitably and forever doomed to be violent. In the last chapter, he and coauthor Dale Peterson offer us as the primary example of an enlightened species the bonobo, a peace-loving, make-love-not-war primate that is also very closely genetically related to humans. Biological determinism is not Wrangham and Peterson's purpose. They end their book with this challenge: "If we are cursed with a demonic male temperament and a Machiavellian capacity to express it, we are also blessed with an intelligence that can, through the acquisition of wisdom, draw us away from the 5-million-year stain of our ape past."

I like the promise, but I disagree that there is an inevitable "animal" stain that comes from having been connected to apes millions of years ago. After all, apes would include gorillas, bonobos, and orangutans—none of whom have even a fraction of the violence that we have seen in chimpanzees.

When Wrangham says the chimps are being cruel, it is worth asking whether we are entitled to make this judgment. There is evidence that animals in general—even bonobos—are not aware that they are being cruel, even when a human observer would definitely consider what is seen to be cruel. Although bonobos are considered vegetarians, some researchers have been shocked to realize that they hunt the tiny, shy duiker, a small antelope. "Duikers were not killed before being eaten, but were opened ventrally at the abdomen while still alive. Consumers stuck their fingers into the opening and licked them. Intestines were eaten first . . . by poking with the index finger, it extracted brain matter through the *foramen magnum*."[12] Pretty gruesome stuff for the animal we have come to see as our role model for "peaceful coexistence." It is hard to believe the bonobos are aware of the suffering they cause. What prevents them from generalizing from their own species to another species is probably the same thing that prevents some humans from making the same leap. Just as the bonobos cannot see what they do to a mere antelope as cruel, so too are many humans unwilling to see that what they do to mere farm animals is also cruel. Species blindness, I would call it.

ANTS CERTAINLY DO something that resembles waging war. Mark Moffett in his book *Adventures among Ants: A Global Safari with a Cast of Trillions* has said, "Among animals, all-out war against their fellows occurs only among the largest societies of humans and ants."

If we are tempted to read into ant wars lessons for humans, it is probably because of the work of E. O. Wilson, and especially his 1975 magnum opus *Sociobiology*, which argues that genes play the ultimate role in human behavior and that traits such as human violence, racism, slavery, and so on can best be explained by biology rather than a person's social environment and passing intellectual fashions. Compared to ant warfare, human war is mild, in his opinion: "If some imaginary Martian zoologist visiting earth were to observe man as simply one more species over a very long period of time, he might conclude that we are among the more pacific mammals." I have to ask, what planet is he living on?

It is hard to deny that some of what ants do bears a striking parallel to a human phenomenon. For example, there is the "dear enemy phenomenon," where ants have established territorial borders and can even go so far as to establish a strip of land that acts as a limbo region between disputed areas of different ant species. Moffett observed this in Argentina between sugar ants and harvester ants.

I am not opposed to learning lessons from other animals, including insects, as long as we realize the limitations, and that applies to my own arguments in this book. So while Wilson and Bert Hölldobler in their magnificent Pulitzer Prize–winning volume *The Ants* don't draw human lessons, it surely is instructive to realize that when an alien species of ant was introduced by humans on

Santa Cruz Island in the Galapagos, it extinguished the populations of every other ant species it encountered, reminding us of nothing so much as the destructive power of colonialism. Recently, in Europe, colonies of a single species of ant were discovered that stretch for 3,700 miles. One might conclude that supercolonies are bad for everyone, ants and humans. For the last five thousand years, at no point has there been a year without some country or faction being at war.

6 · Killing

This animal is black, massive, dangerous with a brutal stupidity . . . viciously decides on his victim . . . he is a beast with only
one idea at a time . . . One pities the stupidity of the animal, it is
a formidable brute stupidity.
>   —V. S. Pritchett, *The Spanish Temper*, writing about bulls

 MANY VIEW THE NATURAL WORLD AS one of "eat or be eaten."
But only 10 percent of mammals are carnivores, maybe
five hundred animal species. The other 90 percent, the
herbivores—forty-five hundred species—may need to be vigilant,
but they need not be aggressive. They may compete for mating
privileges; almost all animals do, but rarely does the competition
end in death (less than 1 percent of the time, my reading of the
literature suggests). Think of chickens, for example. We have a
tendency to believe that chickens are aggressive with one another
and will happily kill another chicken. But this is entirely untrue, as
any number of studies show.[1] So where does this mistaken impression of ours come from? Partly from our belief that roosters are
equipped to kill other roosters.[2] But cockfighting is an entirely
human construct. The roosters are fitted out with spurs, razor-sharp

dagger-like steel blades. These are no more natural to roosters than brass knuckles are to adolescent male gang members.

Though it happens frequently, cockfighting is illegal in all fifty states in the United States.[3] It is an ancient and popular practice in other countries, such as Mexico, the Philippines, Malaysia, and Indonesia. Even though the government has officially banned cock fighting in Bali since 1981, it is ubiquitous and law enforcement is lax, considering it a traditional pastime. People attend for the gambling and the excitement of seeing blood. Women complained to me in Bali that an entire month's salary could easily be lost at a local fight. Men who are addicted to this are called "cock crazy," and there are stories of people who have been reduced to complete poverty because of the craze for betting on fights. By the way, the suggestive pun is just as evident in Balinese as it is in English, and there are endless jokes about Balinese men who identify exclusively with their animal "friend."

Men can be seen walking around during the day paying enormous amounts of attention to their rooster: A man strokes him, speaks to him, massages him, ruffles his feathers every few minutes, and keeps him healthy, vigorous, and well-groomed, paying more attention to his rooster than to his children. I often saw men kissing their rooster on the beak. Anthropologist Clifford Geertz, a leading authority on Balinese cockfighting, notes men would spend inordinate amounts of time "just gazing at them with a mixture of rapt admiration and dreamy self-absorption." However, they'll still cook them for dinner if the bird loses or is fatally injured in a fight. Qualified love, then.

Consider, too, how roosters behave in the wild: they have almost never been seen to fight to the death. They have ritualized battles for territory and for hens, but the loser simply walks away, humiliated, perhaps, but rarely worse for wear. And for most of their existence roosters get on fine with other roosters, simply avoiding one another if necessary. They are not born to fight.

In Bali, I was often told of roosters who did not want to fight and tried to escape the arena, posing a danger to people in the audience, as the poor panicked birds were armed with lethal knives attached to their feet.

It is not only the Balinese but also Geertz himself who regularly ignores the reality of a rooster's life, one of peaceful coexistence. Geertz writes in an essay in *The Interpretation of Culture*, "Most of the time, in any case, the cocks fly almost immediately at one another in a wing-beating, head-thrusting, leg-kicking explosion of animal fury so pure, so absolute, and in its own way so beautiful, as to be almost abstract, a Platonic concept of hate." It's odd that Geertz can write this after acknowledging that hot pepper is put into the anus of the rooster to drive him mad. Refusal to acknowledge the reality of animal behavior under natural conditions is not confined to one anthropologist, one tradition, or one animal. We see it at work in the Spanish bullfight as well.

How similar is cockfighting to bullfighting? There are many parallels. But we are far better equipped to see through the excuses of bullfighting as being a cultural treasure because most of us are more familiar with the arguments. Even today lots of people believe many myths, stereotypes and simply false or distorted views about bulls, especially those used in bullfights. These myths display a dangerous combination of ignorance and arrogance, allowing us to engage in cruel activities toward bulls and then justify our behavior by blaming the bull, branding the animal as cruel. Bulls are domesticated today, and if we raise them to be cruel, it is much like forcing a dog to fight. Our domestic bulls are closely related to wild bulls—for example, the Cape buffalo from Africa. The buffalo herd exists to protect its smaller and weaker members, and the bulls protect the herd. It is such an effective defensive unit that cows who are blind, calves who are lame, and even three-legged bulls who can no longer defend themselves continue to thrive within the herd.[4]

I mentioned earlier how a herd of African Cape buffalo saved a young calf from a pride of lions. The reason so many millions of people have watched this YouTube video is that it illustrates something of which many were completely ignorant: that bulls can be altruistic. Suddenly people saw the bulls in a buffalo herd as heroes, like humans who risk their lives to save a human baby from drowning.

Bulls are not born to fight humans. A wild bull in nature would hardly ever have encountered a human. A domesticated bull has been around people from the time he was born. He is part of a plan, at least five thousand years old, to breed an animal who does not pose a threat to a human. Given the size and weight of cows and bulls, it would be impossible to have them in contact with humans if they were truly wild animals with an inborn natural fear of a predator. In the wild, a human could never approach a wild cow, let alone a wild bull. The animals would simply run off. If they were cornered, they would fight to escape, using their superior strength. But domesticated bulls kept on meadows can quite easily be approached by humans they already know, especially if the bulls have no reason to fear they will be hurt (though bulls can be unpredictable, and strangers should not walk up to them). By and large, bulls are indifferent to humans.

Domesticated bulls are hardly fighting machines. They almost never fight each other, and when they do, it is for access to mating, and is almost always ritualized. The outcome rarely leaves the other male seriously injured. *I do not know of a single authoritative account of two bulls spontaneously fighting to the death.* As for domesticated bulls wanting to kill humans, this is propaganda from the bullfighting industry. The first thing the bull wants, when he enters the ring, is to get out. But there is no escape. Even when the bull has been mortally wounded, he still wants nothing more than to get away. He is trying to defend himself, of course, in the only way he knows; charging a waving flag is merely his way of trying to gain back his equilibrium. He has no animosity toward humans at all until they begin to torture him, and even then, all he wants is for the torture to cease.

Of course the Spanish bullfighting industry does not like this explanation. Those of us who say this are accused of sentimentality. Bulls, we are told, want to fight us. That is why they are called *toros bravos* or *toros de lidia*, that is, fighting bulls or courageous bulls. (That is the true sentimentalism.) Sometimes the apologists will even go so far as to say that bulls are a predator of humans. Needless to say, none of these statements is true.

Consider what happened in 1936 when Munro Leaf published the eight-hundred-word picture book *The Story of Ferdinand.* The book was immediately labeled as subversive antifascist propaganda, burned by Hitler and banned by Franco.[5] In the story, Ferdinand the bull looked ferocious but simply wanted to sit in the field and smell the flowers. Ferdinand became known as "the peaceful bull," an idea considered outrageous by some and propaganda by others. In fact, this was a far more realistic portrait of real bulls than the ones propagated by bullfighters and their fans.

Another myth is that in bullfighting, the fight is fair—the bull has a sporting chance. So what percentage of fights end with the matador's death? In total, fifty-two *matadores de toros* have been killed in the arena since 1700. In two hundred years of bullfighting in a single city, Seville, only thirty fighters have died (and only three were actually matadors). It is estimated that 250,000 bulls are killed *every year* around the world. (In Spain alone, it is 40,000.) And if a bull does kill a fighter, the next matador comes in to kill him. Should a bull kill a human, it was the historical practice to kill the bull's mother, since the evil qualities (defending himself) are assumed to have come from her.

In fact, to call bullfighting a fight at all is a misnomer. It is more like murderous bullying, where a gang of armed thugs is pitted against a lone, terrified, and confused animal forcibly removed from his flock, the only place he feels safe. The continual sounds the bull makes in the pen are really him calling the herd.[6] Once the bull is separated from the herd, already a traumatic and unnatural moment, he is put in a truck for a long, hot ride.[7] Of course, bulls are never housed together, because they would try to protect not only themselves but their herd mates as well. This could pose a danger to humans.

The domesticated bull is a large and powerful animal, one who learns very quickly. So a contest between a bull and a human, if the bull were truly provoked into fighting, would not go well for the unarmed human. No human can run as fast as a healthy adolescent bull.

To create the show of a fight, the bull is wounded and disabled before entering the ring, and is given large amounts of salt to make sure he drinks to the point of being bloated and will move slowly. On the day of the "fight," Vaseline is rubbed into his eyes so he cannot see clearly, and newspaper is stuffed into his ears so he cannot hear properly. Horns are shaved to make them less dangerous and to throw the bull off balance. The muscles in his neck are cut so that he cannot raise his head in normal fashion, which would allow him to see his adversary. His kidneys and testicles are beaten. He is given laxatives, tranquilizers, and drugs to induce paralysis, and other drugs to disorient him. He is kept in total darkness in a tiny cell for at least twenty-four hours, dazed and confused, without food or water (except sulfates, which give him severe diarrhea). You won't find any of this information in Hemingway.

Suddenly the bull is let out into bright sunlight, where he is functionally blind. Bulls hate direct sun and heat. In a field they seek out shade. His first instinct is to race for an exit. Humans have designed the bullring round on purpose, so the bull has no sense of where he came from. We could call this the topography of terror. There are no corners in a bullring, no place for a terrified animal to find refuge. A circular enclosure is unknown to the natural world of the bull.

Great pains are taken to disorient the bull. Men on horseback (picadors) drive long sharp lances into his back to weaken and enrage him. Banderillas, large dagger-like harpoons with colored flags on top, are sunk into his neck and spinal cord causing deep tissue damage and internal hemorrhaging. The bull roars in pain. The bull is terrified, completely unable to understand what is happening or why. Even the shouting of the crowd is completely new, unexpected, and frightening. Often the bulls simply lie down (and the crowds jeer at them as cowards), try to crawl away, or desperately seek an exit. By this time, almost all bulls are urinating and defecating in terror, much like a human just before an execution. As a last resort, some bulls attempt to push away their attacker with their horns. This is *not* an attack, but a final defense.

Sometimes, though, the bull will approach a bullfighter who does not appear to be hostile as if looking for help, or perhaps even mercy. Neither is ever shown. The bull must die.

According to Jared Diamond in the 2008 *New Yorker* article "Vengeance Is Ours," "the thirst for vengeance is among the strongest of human emotions." Whether one agrees or not, clearly history shows how important vengeance has been as a source of strife, murder, and even war. It is almost unheard of in nature.

We accept lightly the notion of hunting for sport and see ourselves as behaving in a natural way, just like other species—just like other apex predators. Yet lions and gazelles are happy to share the grass around a water hole, as long as the lion is not hungry. The big cats do not attack humans unprovoked, unless the cats are ill, old, or incapacitated in some other way. Some leopards even seem to have an affinity for humans and "tame" easily, something we have taken advantage of to create the house cat, one of our only benign domestication gestures.

Nobody would deny that we kill the big cats in enormous numbers, compared with how often they kill us. But there is some dispute as to how much killer instinct these animals actually have, and toward whom it is directed.

Domestic cats definitely seem closer to their wild counterpart than dogs do to wolves. I never ever feel threatened by Benjy, my yellow Lab. But my cats sometimes give me a peculiar look, and I know better than to try to force them to do something they would rather not. No leashes for them. No raised voice. No commands, not even "no." Cats demand a certain distance that Benjy and others of his kind do not. They feel and give love for sure, but at the time and place of their choosing, not necessarily ours. That is why I always feel so privileged when one of my four cats decides to spend the night next to me in bed. We take for granted that dogs want to sleep next to us.

In his book *The Tiger: A True Story of Vengeance and Survival*, John Vaillant tells how in 1997, deep in the remote Russian back-country, a poacher named Markov wounded a gigantic Amur or Siberian tiger.[8] The tiger discovered the man's cabin and dragged a mattress out of his shack so he could lie comfortably in wait until the woodsman returned home. A few days later, the woodsman's horrified friends discovered remains "so small and so few they could have fit in a shirt pocket."

Vaillant notes, "In general, animals (including tigers) avoid conflicts whenever possible because fighting hurts, and the margins in the wild are simply too tight. Most predators—leopards or solitary wolves, for example—will abandon a contested kill rather than risk an injury." I agree, but Vaillant believes that at least the male Amur tiger can be vindictive. He claims, "Amur tigers will occasionally kill bears solely on something that we might recognize as principle."

I have never known any other animal, besides humans, to kill just on principle—that is, because the other belongs to a different species. We don't think of animals, even tigers, as capable of revenge. Animals we keep in captivity, of course, such as orcas and elephants, do feel vengeful toward us, and sometimes kill us.

But in the case of this particular tiger, he really wanted to hunt down the man who tried to kill him. How human. It is highly unusual and risky behavior. On the other hand, Amur tigers can weigh up to eight hundred pounds. There isn't much they are afraid of. So it would appear this tiger was hunting for Markov, his human enemy, the one who had the gall to wound him, with what the people who were aware of it considered alarming confidence and clarity of purpose. How we hate it when the tables are reversed: it is galling to us to suddenly see ourselves as prey. (It is also possible this tiger had the smell of the human and was simply hungry.)

But while tigers kill humans, we would not normally say they prey on us. In the Sundarbans of Bangladesh, 100 to 150 people are killed every year by tigers; in the rest of the world humans are not really part of their diet and tigers avoid us. The reason for the disparity seems to have something to do with tradition. Culture, if you like: tigers see other tigers kill and eat humans and they imitate them. But the comment by Jim Corbett, who was once a lion and tiger hunter, still stands many years later: "A man-eating tiger is a tiger that has been compelled through stress of circumstances beyond its control, to adopt a diet that is alien to it. The stress of circumstances is, in nine cases out of ten, wounds, and in the tenth, old age." Man-eating tigers almost always carry old wounds, often the result of being shot by hunters. Isn't it logical to think the tigers knew they had human predators, and fought back? Tigers killing humans is more or less unknown in Myanmar, Thailand, Malaysia, and Sumatra. In most places on the Indian subcontinent, tigers do not kill humans.

While we may never entirely understand the reason for the

high number of humans killed in the Sundarbans, a successful and remarkably inventive method has been discovered to help end the killings. Since it is known that tigers attack from behind, not face-to-face, the area's eight thousand honey collectors were outfitted with rubber face masks to wear on the back of their heads. The next year, not one person wearing the mask was killed, but twenty-nine people who temporarily removed the masks were. What this shows is that the tigers are merely opportunists. Emotions just do not enter into the picture. If the tigers are convinced they are seen, they do not attempt to kill. The reason has to do with safety: no tiger wishes to engage in risky behavior if he or she might get hurt in the process.

IF LIONS AND tigers rarely kill humans, what about the big cats killing one another? In a book considered the most thorough study of African leopards ever done, Theodore Bailey writes: "Fighting among leopards was rare . . . Actual fighting among highly specialized carnivores is not advantageous to their physical well being and survival."[9] While fighting is uncommon, it has been observed from time to time: "Fights are usually of brief duration and fights seldom result in the death of either of the combatants. Apparently most fights between males occur when one male is attempting to establish himself in an area already occupied by a resident male."

The most elaborate study of lions remains respected naturalist George Schaller's *The Serengeti Lion*, in which there is a description of six lions killed by other lions. Schaller mentions two other authors who also describe instances of lions killing each other. A weird thing about lions is that sometimes the male will chase away females to make certain that cubs eat; at other times, the cubs can actually starve as the adults prevent them from eating after a kill. The *Oxford Encyclopedia of Mammals* acknowledges this behavior, but the editor also points out: "These 'Maneaters of Tsavo' were themselves the victims of human activity, for just a few years earlier Europeans had inadvertently imported a cattle virus that decimated wild ungulates as well as livestock, leaving little for the lions to eat."

Schaller writes about mortality in young lions and adult lions: "Of 23 male and female lions 2 years old and older, resident in the Masai and Seronera prides in June 1966, one male was killed in a fight, another male probably died of wounds incurred in a fight, one female died of old age, a second one, also old, was last seen in poor condition and unquestionably died, and a third female suddenly disappeared with one of her two cubs and possibly was killed by other lions. At the end of 1969 eighteen of the original members were left." In other words, 5.5 percent per year were killed, and Schaller did not see a single instance of a female killed by a male. I think that lions are so well endowed with weapons in their claws that even if they do not intend to kill, a wound can end up killing. I see this in my domestic cats: they can be dangerous because they have such sharp claws and are often bad-tempered. But they definitely intend to scare, not to kill. Meghala will sit on my lap, contentedly purring, until I do something he does not like. Then he does not hesitate to sink his claws into me, even to the point of drawing blood. He doesn't seem to feel bad about it at all, even if I do.

We may well wonder why the big cats tend to be bad-tempered. Here is one of those negative emotions that we *can*, for a change, apply to other animals besides humans. I once tried to make the case that we almost never use the term "sweet-natured" to refer to an adult human male, though we use it frequently for adult male dogs. But "bad-tempered" appears relevant to both adult human males and adult male big cats.

I am beginning to think that the problem with lions is that they are equipped by nature with such lethal tools for one purpose that it is almost impossible not to use them for others. It is like giving a human a machine gun. It goes to his head.

The cats who live with us in our homes tolerate us to an unusual degree for a wild animal. I say wild, because cats remain, to some extent, not entirely domesticated. We can safely say that their behavior is almost identical to that of their wild cousins, the big cats from whom they descend. Not only do they tolerate us, they often seem to like us to an inordinate degree. I need only point you to the incredible story of Christian the lion (which I will explain below) and the phenomenal popularity of the video where in his incarnation as a wild lion once again, he meets up with his two previous human companions. That said, when I first watched the video, I had my heart in my mouth. Here is why: Almost all cats I know will only tolerate you rubbing their tummy to a limited degree. If you go too far, or even if they have just had enough, or if their instincts are aroused, you may well find that your hand is now a prisoner: four paws, with claws out, are holding it. You may try to withdraw it only to find that the more you do so, the deeper the claws go into your hand. You look at your cat with incredulity: "See here, Meghala, it's me, you idiot!" What is he doing? Just being a felid. I have awakened a hunting maneuver in an obligate carni-vore. I should have thought of that before.

Meghala is only five pounds. The average size of a male lion is four hundred pounds. If Meghala jumped up on me with his claws out, I would be alarmed. If he weighed four hundred pounds, I'd be toast. I don't think Meghala intends to harm me. I am sure he does not. Like other cats, after I speak to him soothingly and remind him who I am and where he is (in a house, not in the jungle), he slowly, if somewhat reluctantly, relinquishes his hold on me and lets me go, to live another day.

I give Meghala and the other three cats I live with a lot of respect, and a lot of room. They are still carnivores and quite different from

Benjy, my yellow Labrador retriever, about whom I have written a book with the self-explanatory title *The Dog Who Couldn't Stop Loving*. Push Meghala a bit, and he can easily stop loving you, at least for the moment.

Because of my experience with tiny felines, I was very moved by the story of Christian the lion. Ace Bourke and John Rendall were young Australians in London when they bought a young lion from Harrods department store in 1969. They took him on day trips to the seashore and were something of a major street attraction every time they went out on the town for a walk. When Christian was a year old and growing larger, they realized a lion could never be happy in London and got in touch with the Kenyan conservationist George Adamson (of *Born Free* fame). George took Christian to the Kora National Reserve in Kenya. There he became the head of a lion pride in the wild.

In 1972 Ace and John decided they wanted to visit this site and see if they could locate their old friend. They traveled to Kenya, and a photographer was present when they found their former companion. It is an inspiring if terrifying moment. The film shows the lion cautiously approach his two old friends. Then suddenly he realizes who they are, and he leaps up joyfully, wrapping his huge front legs around their shoulders and nuzzling their faces in the excitement of his recognition. He is profoundly happy to see them, of that there can be no doubt. It's incredibly moving to see Christian the lion lunge at his friends Ace and John with pure joy in his heart, a full year after he was released in the African savannah. Evidently Christian—who had, after all, been a tame lion at one point in his life—was able to convince his female companions, Mona and Lisa, who were not tame at all, to indulge his human friends as well, permitting them to visit and stroke their cubs, one of whom, Supercub, welcomed the two men as well.

We are simply not accustomed to seeing a fully wild animal

express friendship and love for a member of another species, and one who is a predator, even a predator of his species. It defies our sense of ourselves: we should be the only animal capable of this feat. Yet (of course) we are not.

With an animal as formidably armed by nature as any of the great cats, it may well be that they do not mean to kill you, it's a case of involuntary manslaughter. They lack intent, but you are in the way. I would suggest this is true of intraspecies violence as well: lions just want to drive other lions away.

In *The Carnivores*, E. R. Ewer, the leading scholar on the subject, has written what I believe is a major insight into the nature of carnivore violence: "Possibly the most striking feature of carnivore social organization is the rarity with which serious fighting appears to be required in 'maintaining law and order.'" The animals, she explains, respect "ownership," and one carnivore simply passing through does not try to take over from the established owner and in return is rarely challenged, in fact is mostly given free passage.[10]

Schaller, too, had the impression that in a chase, a lion in pursuit of another lion was taking good care not to catch up with his quarry. He was seeing him off rather than trying to catch him. This is why lions roar: to warn other males that someone is already there. "If every skirmish between male lions," Schaller notes, "were to escalate into a raging battle the animals could suffer lethal wounds. By roaring instead males are able to signal their dominance and avoid incurring injuries."[11]

The puma (the term preferred by scientists, but also called cougars in the eastern United States—even though almost none live there—and mountain lions in California) is the same animal as the panther or leopard in the Old World. They are known to be shy, and while females stay with their mothers, males are pretty much solitary. They are also aggressive: I was told by Ken Logan, one of America's leading puma field biologists, that up to half of cougar deaths can be attributed to attacks by other cougars, almost always males. They travel alone, almost never in pairs, and certainly never in packs. The reason for this is that their nutritional needs are so high that a male cougar needs a home range estimated to be between thirty-six and four hundred square miles. Logan did not see any evidence of fighting between females. Sometimes, for reasons not fully understood, males killed females and cannibalized their young. Still, Ken Logan says that trophy hunting is by far the single greatest mortality factor for lions throughout the West (where they live almost exclusively, but for about a hundred still in Florida).

Cougars kill humans, but rarely. Between 1890 and 1989, in the United States and Canada, records show a total of thirty-six attacks, eleven of which resulted in human deaths. Of the fifteen cats—all of whom were later killed—a full 80 percent were sick or underweight.

Rick Hopkins, a cougar biologist who has studied the cats in the Diablo Mountains of northern California, says the risk of an attack is one in twenty-five million. So when the poet Gary Snyder writes, "The wild is perhaps the very possibility of being eaten by a mountain lion," we have to take this as poetic license. In their authoritative book *Wild Cats of the World*, Mel and Fiona Sunquist write: "Like cheetahs, pumas are gentle, retiring cats, more eager to flee than fight, and both species rarely confront humans." (Though we have seen that they are not so gentle when it comes to one another, and this view is not accepted by all researchers.)

A man-eating leopard in India in the 1920s was thought to have killed 125 people. After the Indian army sent a company of Gurkha soldiers to kill the feared "beast" but returned without success, the British Parliament asked Jim Corbett, a famed big-cat hunter, to find and kill the leopard. He finally succeeded in 1925. In his book

The Man-Eating Leopard of Rudraprayag, Corbett notes: "Here was only an old leopard, who differed from others of his kind in that his muzzle was grey and his lips lacked whiskers; the best-hated and the most feared animal in all India, whose only crime—not against the laws of nature, but against the laws of man—was that he had shed human blood with no object of terrorizing man, but only in order that he might live."

These animals are acting out of character only because they have been traumatized. For a predator to become prey is definitely a trauma, for humans or for other animals. Even then, these other animals act only to satisfy basic needs. Humans are the only species that will act out fantasies putting themselves and others in danger out of pure paranoia. Paranoia is strictly a human condition.

It is, when you think about it, extraordinary that we are *not* prey for most apex predators, including orcas and sperm whales, the largest predator who has ever lived on earth. Richard Wrangham has pointed out that fighting adults of almost all species normally stop at winning: Only humans will fight on, even when there is nothing to be gained by the killing.

BUT ARE WE really "man the hunter," as was believed in the 1960s? Donna Hart, in an article in the *Chronicle of Higher Education* entitled "Humans as Prey," points out that humans were hardly "the toughest kids on the block" for the vast majority of their time on earth. Quite the contrary—we were more like the ninety-pound weakling, she says. She and others believe, and I agree, that an urge to cooperate with one another, even if only to help avoid predators, is built in: "Deadly competition among individuals or nations may be highly aberrant behavior, not hard-wired survival techniques."[12] There is hope for us after all.

Darwin, alas, insisted that hunting in our evolutionary history explained the innate superiority of men over women: "To avoid enemies, or to attack them with success, to capture wild animals, and to invent and fashion weapons, requires the aid of the higher mental faculties, namely, observation, reason, invention, or imagination. These various faculties will thus have been continually put to the test, and selected during manhood ... Thus man has ultimately become superior to women" (*The Descent of Man*).

No other animal is burdened with such misinformation, prejudices, and clichés of their culture. Odd to think that swans know more about equality than Darwin. To see just how pernicious this has been, consider how Robert Ardrey in his influential book *The Hunting Hypothesis* about man as killer ape summed up his thesis: "If among all the members of our primate family the human being is unique, even in our noblest aspirations, it is because we alone through untold millions of years were continuously dependent on killing to survive." Not only does this distort human history, but it misrepresents animals as well. The truth is very different, as we shall see.

7 · Hatred

I couldn't possibly write *Jaws* today . . . the notion of demonizing a fish strikes me as insane.

—Peter Benchley

HATRED IS A PECULIAR EMOTION; IT is like the distillation left in the wake of anger. But anger is temporary and can be benign. Hatred is, by definition, something that lasts and is meant to invoke or provoke more than feelings. It seems like a call to action: if we hate somebody, we want to harm that person, or if we are civilized, we don't wish to actually harm the object of our enmity, but we would not mind if harm were to come to the person. Or if we are a better person than that, perhaps, we just cannot help enjoying the thought of his or her misfortune. Only a saint feels none of these things, but saints are theoretical beings, not flesh and blood. All of us have felt hate. The Buddha is supposed to have said, "There is no shark like hatred," but the Buddha probably never saw a shark and seems never to have hated. So how would he know?[1]

Every example of extreme violence I have written about in this book is connected to hatred. This is often denied: people speak too lightly of the "banality of evil," meaning that it is possible to inflict great harm upon people without experiencing anything resembling hatred. This is a pernicious idea, and I don't believe it for one moment. Just as when we help people we experience a degree of solidarity that involves affection and liking, so too when we harm somebody we experience a degree of dislike or at least indifference.

The other day I was talking to a popular divorce attorney who works in the Washington, D.C., area. He told me that after forty years of practicing this kind of law, he still couldn't get used to the extraordinary hatred his clients feel for the one person they once loved beyond all others.

Neuroscientists claim that the same brain centers are activated by love and hatred. This is possible, but surely there are no neurological roots for the most dangerous form of hatred, which also happens to be the most common: group hatred, or, rather, hatred of a large group of people. This form of loathing is related far more to learned prejudices than to brain structure. Both forms of hatred are important to humans, and they are such visible and frequent emotions that we simply assume they must play an equally large role in the lives, both outer and inner, of other animals. But this is rather a uniquely human emotion. A predator does not hate his prey. Getting food is serious business for all animals, and that business becomes dangerous when hunting is involved. There is no room for emotions such as pity or hatred, which would merely get in the way of a job that needs doing. There is of course pleasure in the hunt, just as there is pleasure in eating.

In any artificial battle conceived by humans—those fought in Roman amphitheaters, for example—we are forced to invent motives for the combatants. Machismo is a quality exclusively attributable to human animals. There are no macho animals in nature.

We are so used to taking things personally, with good reason, that it is hard for us to acknowledge that when we become prey there are no hard feelings on the part of the predator. There is a terrifying scene from the film *Saving Private Ryan* where a German soldier is as frightened as his American counterpart but wins a hand-to-hand combat and slowly pushes in the knife that will kill the American. As he does so, he tells the American to hush and accept the inevitable. He behaves like a mother comforting her child before a painful operation. The point of the scene is to show that this is war and he is doing what he must do, but it is without hatred, in fact, quite the contrary—the German recognizes that the man he kills is just like him, a human being. That is why the film is called an antiwar film.

THAT PREY ANIMALS feel extraordinary fear, even terror, is likely, just as we would if hunted down for sport or food. They feel pain as much or more than we do and want to live just as much.[2] Do animal predators, though, feel anything negative toward their prey? I doubt it. There is good evidence that when sharks are well fed, as in an aquarium, they swim without showing the least aggression either to other fish or to human divers cleaning the tanks.

It is difficult for us to empathize with sharks.[3] We are terrified of them. But where does this terror come from? Some of it no doubt goes back to the release of Peter Benchley's phenomenally successful novel *Jaws*. The book and film created a tremendous panic about swimming in the ocean. If we look to evolutionary psychology, we'll find an attempt to explain everything in terms of the human evolutionary past. But how many great white sharks did humans encounter in their early history? Very few. Yet a fear of sharks is almost universal, and most would say it is innate. Does that mean we are born with such a fear or that everyone acquires such a fear easily?

WE HUMANS SEE ourselves as the supreme predator of all other apex predators, so what happens when we become prey? Enter the great white shark—the greatest killing machine of all natural history, as adolescent boys enjoy telling one another. (The Australian box jellyfish is far more deadly and kills more people, but it does not have much evocative power and therefore no cachet.) However, contrary to what most of us imagine, we are rarely the intended prey of sharks. Sharks, like *all* other apex predators, take only their designated prey as food.

Of course, in the case of sharks, as elsewhere, there is an important connection between our warped interpretation of ourselves as prey and our actions as predators. *Savage Predator of the Sea*, reads the title of one recent book about sharks. This would be a far more appropriate description of humans. We kill sharks not only because we fear them but also because in some societies serving shark-fin soup is a matter of social prestige. Sharks display nothing remotely as irrational as this.

Having said this, it bears repeating that when recently our neighbor saw a great white about half a mile offshore of our house on the beach, nobody wanted to go into the water. True, the chances of being attacked were minuscule, but something prevented us from entering the water until we were sure, a few days later, that the shark had moved on. Perhaps it was something primitive in *our* brain, but it was pretty universal, at least on our beach. Shortly thereafter our family went for a vacation to a popular beach south of Auckland. As we were all catching waves, somebody noticed a shark, maybe three or four feet long. We all exited the water rather rapidly and watched the shark swimming just a few feet away. It was, as my then nine-year-old-son Manu said, "awesome." But we stayed out of the water the rest of the day.

The great white shark is only one of 375 species of shark, most of them harmless. Only thirty species of sharks have ever been known to attack people, and most of those attacks are by just three specific kinds: the great white shark, the bull shark, and the tiger shark. However, no animal works on the human imagination with quite the same malign power as the great white shark—even though the chances of anyone being attacked by this apex predator are exceedingly remote. Just how dangerous are sharks to humans? Even if we consider only people who go to beaches, a person's chance of being killed by a shark is less than 1 in 264 million. In the United States, about three thousand people drown every year, and more than sixteen thousand people are murdered. But, on average, every year a shark kills one person, possibly for food, possibly by accident, or in a case of mistaken identity. (Divers often look like seals with their dark wet suits.)

Some estimates put the number of sharks killed by humans at a hundred million every year. That works out to roughly eleven thousand sharks every hour, around the clock, including tens of millions for their fins alone.

It had been commonly assumed that sharks, being fish, cannot have any feelings, or much of a brain. But this view is seriously outdated. Writing in the journal *Fish and Fisheries*, biologists Calum Brown, Kevin Laland, and Jens Krause made the following comment:

> Gone (or at least obsolete) is the image of fish as drudging and dim-witted pea brains, driven largely by "instinct," with what little behavioral flexibility they possess being severely hampered by an infamous "three-second memory". . . . Now, fish are regarded as steeped in social intelligence, pursuing Machiavellian strategies of manipulation, punishment and reconciliation, exhibiting stable cultural traditions, and co-operating to inspect predators and catch food.

As with most animals, the more we learn, the more we need to overturn old prejudices, biased views, misinformation, ignorance, and sheer stupidity, even when it comes to fish. We do somewhat better the more closely the animal resembles us, but this is just one further instance of our own narcissism.

In 1991, the South African government declared the great white shark a protected species. Louis Pienaar, the minister for environmental affairs, in making the announcement, said that, encouraged by the film *Jaws*, trophy hunters were targeting great whites in South African waters, convinced the great white was a ruthless man-eater to be eliminated. This would no longer be tolerated. The need for protecting sharks, even the great white, and recognizing that they were not a threat to us (on the contrary, we were a threat to them) constituted an enlightened view at the time. It is now pretty commonly accepted as true.

Peter Benchley himself acknowledged that his information was erroneous, and he tried to make amends. He wrote, "It is widely accepted that sharks in general, and great whites in particular, do not target human beings." He went further in a remarkable mea culpa, admitting how badly he had misunderstood sharks out of pure ignorance.

Maybe something else about sharks makes them occupy such a prominent place in our psyches. They are the only wild predator that cannot be tamed. People have lived with lions, wolves, tigers, boa constrictors, rhinos, orcas, wild boars, dolphins, hippos, and just about any other animal you can think of, but nobody has ever lived on intimate terms with a great white shark. Barracudas can be "gentled" and birds of prey are easily tamed. Stingrays may nestle in the palm of your hand like a butterfly and delicately eat from your fingers, but no one has tried anything similar with a great white. Perhaps it's simply obvious that you do not attempt to tame an animal with three thousand razor-sharp teeth. All of this new

information and our new dawning respect yield yet more reasons
to abandon any idea of hating these animals simply because they
are unlike us and sometimes, even if mistakenly, take us for prey.
Hatred for us plays no role in the sharks' lives, and hatred for them
should play none in ours.

You could also take a more philosophical approach, the one that
Don Reed, a diver at Marine World/Africa USA, took when his
"friendship" with an eight-foot sevengill shark came to an abrupt
end. After years of being together without incident, the shark took
his head in her massive jaws. Said Reed, "If Sevengill was abso-
lutely no monster, neither was she on this earth to be my pet." He
was lucky to have lived. Taking wild animals as pets is never a good
idea, and we should not be angry if the animals think so as well.
Any animal not domesticated is a poor candidate for living with
humans. They have their own rules of behavior and are unlikely to
bend to ours. Tragedies occur often when people forget or refuse to
acknowledge our "separateness."

Are we doomed to hate apex predators because they are, like us,
dangerous? I think we can make an interesting distinction between
animals who are solitary, such as several of the big cats, sharks, and
bears, and animals who are sociable, including wolves, whales, and
lions. Could sociable predators be less likely to target animals,
including us, that they see as similar to themselves?

Bears, like sharks, do not regard us as the enemy, though well
they might. They don't really want anything to do with us. Their
experience at the hands of humankind has not been a good one.
Canadian naturalist Charlie Russell's encounter illustrates how
bears are traumatized:

One time, I came across one grizzly female with two cubs down
by the river. When she saw me, she got spooked, but then I
started talking with her and begged her not to leave. I was so

upset that she was so afraid—automatically so frightened that she felt compelled to leave even though she needed food for herself and the cubs badly. I even got on my knees and pleaded for her to relax and come back. She was standing cross-wind to me which meant she could not smell my scent. After a few moments of listening to me, she stopped and brought the cubs out back across the creek. Bit by bit the grizzly came closer and [all the] while I talked to her. She really looked like she was relaxing. Then she decided to figure out who this guy really was, and walked at right angles to smell me. She came across the water so that the wind was at my back. Then suddenly, she hit my scent and a ripple flashed through her muscles. It was like a club had hit her. She was instantly afraid. The mother bear tore back, picked up the cubs and ran away across the river. She was in absolute terror. I felt like weeping. What was it in her memory that made her so scared by human scent? Was it something that she experienced? Did she witness her mother killed in front of her and smell the men who had killed her? Or even worse, have humans been so violent to bears that their fear of people has become genetic memory? (Available on kerulos.org/projects/t-s-grizzlies.html)

For no apparent reason, we kill thousands of bears every year. Nobody knows the exact number, but the Humane Society of the United States estimates that hunters legally kill at least thirty-three thousand bears every year. Poachers kill thousands more.

On average, bears kill about one human a year.[4] In 2009 Kelly Ann Walz, thirty-seven, of Ross Township, Pennsylvania, was attacked as she cleaned her "pet" bear's cage. She also had a Bengal tiger and a lion in her backyard. Donna Munson, seventy-four, was feeding bears on her property in southwestern Colorado when one ate her instead. That same year, California's Department of Fish and Game reported that 1,900 black bears had been "harvested." In Virginia, the number was 2,204. And just to keep a little perspective, note that also in 2009, 15,241 Americans met their death at the hands of other people.[5]

PEOPLE WHO CLAIM to love bears and would not dream of killing one have no problem putting them into the prisons we call zoos. What do we believe we achieve when we put a polar bear on display in a zoo, only to drive him mad? A polar bear can easily roam a thousand miles in a year (up to fifty miles in a single day); in the zoo, polar bears spend a quarter of their entire time pacing back and forth, *trying to get out.* Most of the cubs born to polar bear mothers in zoos die immediately. The lesson is clear: it is a crime against nature to keep them there.[6]

But what most people want to hear about bears is how very dangerous they are. Hence the popularity of Stephen Herrero's marvelous *Bear Attacks: Their Causes and Avoidance.*

Yes, grizzlies are dangerous, but to whom? Consider Werner Herzog's film *Grizzly Man,* which recounts the true story of Timothy Treadwell. Treadwell spent twelve years with the grizzlies in Alaska, shooting one hundred hours of extraordinary video footage at close range. His website (www.grizzlypeople.com—still up and running as of July 2013) warns against getting closer than a hundred yards to a bear, yet he was often right up in their faces, even touching their noses with his finger. Bad idea. (Bears do not allow other bears to touch them—they are very much like cats in this respect.)

There is little doubt that he adored the grizzlies he knew, but it is unlikely that they adored him in return. This is a difficult idea for humans to swallow. If we love an animal, we expect to be loved in return. Still, I would not go so far as Herzog did when he says, "What haunts me is that in all the faces of all the bears that

Treadwell ever filmed, I discover no kinship, no understanding, no mercy. I see only the overwhelming indifference of nature. To me, there is no such thing as a secret world of the bears. And this blank stare speaks only of a half-bored interest in food. But for Timothy Treadwell, this bear was a friend, a savior."

Basically *all* wild animals are indifferent to us. We are accustomed to our domesticated cats, dogs, and other "pets" who do, in fact, adore us in return. Dogs actually love us *more* than we love them (more even than they love themselves), possibly the only such instance in nature. So we may easily make the mistake of falsely projecting a sort of dog love onto other animals. Treadwell spoke to the grizzlies exactly as we speak to our dogs. But the grizzlies were not wagging their tails, jumping for joy, and eager to lick his face in adoration. Sure enough, in 2003, just minutes after filming, Treadwell and his girlfriend, Amie Huguenard (who did *not* want to be there), were attacked and killed by a male grizzly. Nick Jans, in his book on Treadwell, makes the point that the bears "couldn't care less about human trust or physical affection. They're too busy being themselves and are at best indifferent to our existence unless we insinuate ourselves into their lives."[7] It's a hard lesson for any of us.[8]

We need to keep in mind that Treadwell was killed by a bear he did not know and who did not know him, who had been previously tagged and possibly harassed, and who had good reason to feel a grudge against humans. It was the end of October, at the tail end of a very bad berry season, so the bears were hungry and in a bad mood. They were preparing to den with insufficient food. Treadwell and his friend may have simply been in the wrong place at the wrong time.

We have very strong views about bears because they resemble us in many ways. As a recent article put it:

The bear is a large and dangerous carnivore. However, fear alone does not account for the rich and varied traditions linking bears and humans. Not infrequently, people have felt a kind of kinship with bears, for humans and bears share many characteristics. They live in the same regions and eat the same fish, roots, and berries. Unlike other animals, bears can stand on their hind legs as humans do and they can use their fore paws as humans use their hands. A bear's skinned body looks human, and several bear bones resemble human bones, which lends credence to the view that the animal is really a man in disguise.[9]

To the Native Americans—for example, the Lakota, Blackfoot, and Shoshone—bears occupied a special position of honor because of these similarities. The Cherokee, Crow, Yavapi, and other Native Americans thought bears and humans could be transformed into one another.

While bears resemble humans in some ways, in others they are like über-humans. Polar bears, for example, are very large. In fact, polar bears are the largest land meat-eater, three or four times bigger than a big tiger. An adult male polar bear can be nearly ten feet tall and weigh more than fifteen hundred pounds. Slow, though, right? Alas, their top speed running on all fours has been reported to be around 40 mph. Usain Bolt, the fastest man on earth, has a peak speed of 27 mph. You will not outrun the bear.

You don't want to tangle with a bear. In a balanced world, the two species would hardly come into contact. But since industrial development has accelerated climate change, the bears are not finding as much food as they need. So they come into populated areas such as Churchill, Manitoba, on Hudson Bay, a town known as the Polar Bear Capital of the World. One thousand residents, one thousand polar bears.

The town has what is known as the "bear police" to protect tourists and residents. They catch bears wandering into town and put them in a "polar bear jail" until the ice freezes, at which point the bear police fly them by helicopter and drop them onto the ice so that the bears can hunt and find food on their own. If there are problems with bears, we are the ones who have created these problems.

One often reads that polar bears are one of the only animal species known in rare cases to hunt humans, especially when undernourished, frightened, or provoked.[10] However, Tony Smith, a polar bear expert at Brigham Young University, noted that if bears stalk and hunt humans, "they're doing a pretty poor job of it." In the 125 years prior to 2008, polar bears had killed just eight people in Canada and two in Alaska.[11]

So if bears kill humans only infrequently, how common is it for bears to kill other bears? In 2009 I could find no authenticated account of an adult bear killing another adult bear. I am not saying it never happens (we are not likely to be there to witness it when it does), but bear researchers agree it is rare. Like most of the big cats, bears are pretty much solitary creatures. Bears are extremely well endowed with lethal equipment in their claws and jaws, but unlike cats, they cannot pull their claws in. Given that both the big cats and the big bears are of uneven temperament and can get into a bad mood faster than you can say "Let's get out of here now," it is not surprising that they tend to avoid one another. Bears rarely fight one another, probably because the likelihood of mutual injury is so great. Like any solitary animal, they do meet up with their own kind for various reasons, and when they do, they have a very easily recognized means of distinguishing seniority: being big counts for a lot with bears. "Bears may turn to present their profile or stand on their hind legs in order to appear larger and more intimidating." They hiss, they pop their jaws, they yawn, and they swing their head. Humans need to recognize the warning signals to steer clear of these majestic animals; otherwise, bears will often charge. Yet they normally stop short of actual contact. They just want to show who's boss.

Bears may not have room in their lives for camaraderie, certainly not as much as many humans do. On the other hand, they have even less room in their lives for hatred. They can be annoyed, they can be angry, but it is highly unlikely that they feel anything akin to hatred. Even though we give them plenty of reason to hate our species, it appears they do not do so, perhaps because all their energy is needed to survive. Why does hatred play such a prominent role in the lives of that superior species known as *Homo sapiens sapiens*?

8 · Exploitation

Greed is good.

—Gordon Gekko (played by Michael Douglas), in *Wall Street*

AT THE END OF BARRY UNSWORTH'S remarkable novel about slavery, *Sacred Hunger*, a humane surgeon on board a slave ship says: "I knew we had done them harm beyond reckoning . . . It was impossible to pretend otherwise. It was impossible not to see that we had taken everything from them and only for the sake of profit—that sacred hunger, as Delblanc once called it, which justifies everything, sanctifies all purposes." His is a bleak vision, for he notes, "Nothing a man suffers will prevent him inflicting suffering on others. Indeed, it will teach him the way." Slavery lasted hundreds of years, all over the globe, and in every single case it was driven by pure greed.[1]

Slavery and many other institutionalized evils are a product of greed and its twin, greed for power. (The Greeks had a useful word for it, *pleonexia*, an overreaching desire for more than one's share).[2] We want more than our fair share of territory, wealth, oil, and resources in general. And we are willing to engage in lethal combat to get it, at an individual level and at a national level.

No other animal exhibits anything remotely resembling greed as we know it. It is my belief that the origin of greed can be dated to the advent of what we call "civilization."

Not everyone, of course, agrees that we were better off before civilization. When Darwin met people he considered uncivilized, who he thought would correspond to early humans—humans of, say, some thirty thousand years ago—he had unpleasant things to say about them. In *The Voyage of the Beagle*, he recounts meeting people in Tierra del Fuego and not being impressed. While acknowledging that they belonged to the same species, he thought they were, in his words, no better than animals:

> The language of these people, according to our notions, scarcely deserves to be called articulate . . . We have no reason to believe that they perform any sort of religious worship . . . The different tribes have no government or chief . . . They cannot know the feeling of having a home, and still less that of domestic affection . . . Their skill in some respects may be compared to the instinct of animals, for it is not improved by experience.[3]

Darwin was wrong about their language, which is as sophisticated and complex as any other language; indeed, one of the cornerstones of modern linguistics is that all languages are equal.[4] As for their performing no religious worship, neither did Darwin, though he tried to hide this from his religious wife and relatives. And what exactly is wrong with egalitarianism? Since when does having no chief count against you? He also disdained the fact that Fuegians wandered, just as our ancestors did before they had homes they needed to defend against others. Darwin based his comment that they know no domestic affection on hearsay. As for their skills in building, et cetera, one can only guess that he saw far too little of them to know much about the extent of their capacities (he was there less than two weeks). No doubt they could survive in environments in which he could not. Just like animals. And just like animals, we humans had once survived, for many thousands of years, in environments that we did not destroy or pollute or bring to the verge of total collapse.

It is worth asking: does anyone really want to go back to a state of nature, no matter how innocent and how nonviolent, instead of what we have today? I can remember talking with Helena Norberg-Hodge, who opened up the Western appreciation for Ladakh, a region of India. Her point of view was that a rural, simple Buddhist society is preferable to what Ladakh has become more recently. (She explains this in her award-winning film *The Economics of Happiness*.) Her earlier film and book, *Ancient Futures*, presents an almost idyllic world, where everyone had enough home-grown or gathered food and lived in beautiful homes they built themselves out of local materials; it was a world where old people were valued and participated happily in community life, where young people were not alienated, the landscape was unpolluted, and several religious groups lived together in harmony. When Helena asked residents where the poor people lived, she was told there were no poor people (nor was there any money). A few short years later, after the advent of tourism and TV, the importation of cheap food, and the newly instilled desire for a Western lifestyle, it is a culture transformed. For the first time in Ladakh there is crime, poverty, people living in ugly barracks, arguments and fights among the followers of different religions, and air and water unfit to breathe or drink. (See her website, www.localfutures.org.)

Still, I feel sympathy for the young people who tell her that they don't want to go back to simple farming life in their simple village. That said, there is something very compelling about living a life without endless desires, without wanting more and more. While we talk of greed and deplore its ubiquity, few of us are eager to forgo creature comforts.

A turning point that got us on our current path was ten thousand years ago, give or take a few thousand years, when humans opted for two major changes in the way our species evolved: we decided to cultivate plants and to tame animals—agriculture and domestication.

Terra nullius, the idea that a place is empty until "settled," is one of the most destructive concepts in history. The term is notorious in Australia, where in 1971 Justice Richard Blackburn ruled that all of Australia had been *terra nullius* before European settlement and that "natives" had no claim on their own land.[5] This was in accord with English common law, which spoke of legal settlement of "barbarous" country. (The *Mabo* case overturned this law in 1992.) John Locke in his *Two Treatises on Government* (1690) claimed that "natives" had "declared war against all mankind, and therefore may be *destroyed as a lion or tiger, one of those wild savage beasts with whom men can have no society or security*" (italics in original).[6]

The same false notion is at work when humans regard land inhabited *only* by animals to be uninhabited. But this idea became possible only when land under cultivation (agriculture) was considered superior to land, such as forests or jungle, that "belonged" to other species. We did not have this foolish notion when we were hunter-gatherers.

ACCORDING TO ANTHROPOLOGISTS Richard Borshay Lee and Irven DeVore, we are now living in what they call a "brief transitional phase of human history—a phase which included the rise of agriculture, animal domestication, tribes, states, cities, empires, nations, and the industrial revolution." Writing in 1968, they feared this could lead to the complete extinction of our species. In the past ten years we have seen how this could come about: we are destroying rain forests at an extraordinary rate in order to plant soybeans to feed animals, whom we then consume to the detriment of our own health. It is a vicious cycle that has no parallel to our evolutionary history. We are ruining our environment, our health, and the animals around us. It is not necessary and should stop.

While Lee and Devore pay lip service to the simultaneous rise of the domestication of animals, they do not spell out the negative consequences of this process. To borrow Jared Diamond's phraseology, I would call domestication "the second worst mistake in the history of the human race." In his book *An Unnatural Order*, the animal rights activist and attorney Jim Mason was the first scholar to point out what happened once we so cavalierly accepted domestication. In one of his more recent articles, Mason points out that domesticated animals were "castrated, yoked, harnessed, hobbled, penned, [and] shackled, and their sex lives controlled for human gain." We saw them more with contempt than with awe, as had previously been the case.[7]

David Brion Davis, in his book *Inhuman Bondage: The Rise and Fall of Slavery in the New World*, was able to show how animal domestication was deeply involved in the rise of human slavery. It is even possible, in my view, that the very idea of "the other" as somebody without value could be traced back to animal domestication.

I HAVE ALWAYS been a bit reluctant to accept the "wisdom" of native peoples when it comes to their attitudes to the animals they hunt for food. While they may accord them respect, they nonetheless end up killing them. But I have changed my mind about early human hunting. A culture in which there are purification rites before a hunt, or in which the hunters beg the animal for forgiveness before they set out on the hunt, seems to me on the right track. The culture recognizes that the killing may be necessary for survival, but it is to be taken mighty seriously. Surely this is a much better message than to pretend it does not happen at all (Western denial of the slaughterhouse) or to pretend that we really don't have any obligation to reduce animal suffering (hence the inhumane practices of modern agribusiness).

My position is that we no longer need to kill animals at all, whether for food or for any other reason. Today we can recognize that whether we kill with reverence or with indifference, the result to the animal is the same. In the past we could justify this killing as necessary for our survival. No longer.

In *Of Wolves and Men*, Barry Lopez describes this older view about hunting among the Naskapi people of the Labrador peninsula in eastern Canada:

> The agreement is mythic in origin, made with an Owner of the Animals. In the Naskapi world this is the Animal Master of the caribou because the caribou is the mainstay of the Naskapi diet. The Animal Master is a single animal in a great mythic herd. He is both timeless and indestructible, an archetype of the species. It is he who "gives the animal to the hunter to be killed" and who has the power to keep the animals away from the hunter if he is unworthy.

It didn't really matter whether the hunters actually believed in the Animal Master; they were to behave as if they did. This implies that they could not demonstrate cruelty or waste, or even any kind of aggression of the mind. They were hunting to feed their family.

Today, if we feel guilt and recognize how much agony an animal suffers, and that each animal killed valued his or her life as much as we do, we can become people who don't eat animals or their products. Our ancestors did not have this privilege. Jim Mason notes this primal guilt in *An Unnatural Order*:

> If primal people had such feelings and ideas about animals, how could they hunt, kill, and eat them? . . . They viewed prey animals as equals and, in some cases, as kin. An Eskimo hunter's statement reveals this feeling: "The greatest peril in life lies in the fact that human food consists entirely of souls. All the creatures that we have to kill and eat, all those that we have to strike down and destroy to make clothes for ourselves, have souls, like we have, souls that do not perish with the body, and which must therefore be propitiated lest they should avenge themselves on us for taking away their bodies."

Akira Kurosawa's 1975 film *Dersu Uzala* presents this same view in a Nanai native hunter from the last century in far eastern Siberia. It is based on a book written by the Russian explorer Vladimir Arseniev in 1923 as a tribute to Uzala, who lived from 1850 to 1908 and regarded the animals he hunted for sustenance with nothing short of reverence (which he even extended to trees). Arseniev's tough Russian soldiers make fun of the diminutive naïf, mocking him for his animism, but slowly Uzala gains their respect, as he has wisdom about survival that comes from a place they can only guess at. At the end, he briefly lives with Arseniev and his family, who treat him with great kindness, but Uzala longs for his free life in the forest. It is a remarkably melancholy film (Kurosawa killed himself shortly after directing it), in which it becomes clear what "civilized" people lose as they distance themselves from a simpler and more direct life. Uzala in the film is portrayed as the last of the hunter-gatherers.

According to the zoologist James Serpell, this view is common in native cultures:

Although it varies in detail from place to place, the undercurrent of guilt and the need for some form of atonement for animal slaughter is common among hunting people. In certain African tribes, for example, hunters are obliged to undergo ceremonial acts of purification in order to remove the stain of murder from their consciences. In others, the hunter will beg the animal for forgiveness so that it doesn't bear a grudge. The Barasana Indians of Colombia regard the act of killing animals as spiritually dangerous, and believe that their flesh is poisonous unless ritually purified first ... Among the Moi of Indochina, expiatory offerings are made for any animal killed by hunters, because they believe that it has been taken by force from its spiritual guardian who may decide to seek revenge.

From this evidence, Jim Mason concludes: "As bands grew into tribes and populations grew more dense, these hunter cults and hunt rituals grew into warrior cults and war rituals. Both had in common rituals involving painful initiation rites, mutilation, and desensitization to cruelty and suffering—values that survive in masculine culture today. Hunter societies tended to develop these 'strengths' probably as part of preparations for the hunt or for battle."

I believe that a further step was taken once animals were brought into total submission via confinement. Here I part company with those people doing research on domestication who believe this is a process in which animals somehow gave their consent to be domesticated in return for food and protection. That is a myth concocted by humans to make us feel better.

IT DIDN'T HAVE to be this way. Think of dogs. The eminent paleoarchaeologist Pat Shipman believes that dogs have been with us for at least thirty-five thousand years.[8] Others (Robert K. Wayne and colleagues from the Department of Genetics at the University of California, Los Angeles) believe it is even longer, perhaps a hundred thousand years.[9] If we compromise and come up with a figure of fifty thousand years, that means our canine companions have been at our side basically since we were modern humans—*Homo sapiens sapiens*.[10] Whether dogs chose to come to us or we encouraged them against their better judgment, they became essential to human society. Some scientists claim that the reason we surpassed the Neanderthals is that we had dogs and they did not. Dogs performed many useful services: guarding us, warning us of danger from other animals or other humans, keeping us warm, hunting with us, eating our garbage, and so on. I also believe they were our friends from early on (although some societies repaid their love for us by eating them).

I spend time watching humans interact with their dogs, and I spend part of my day interacting with my own dog, and I know that we get enormous pleasure from stroking them, talking to them, walking with them, interacting with them on an emotional level, and, yes, loving them. What is more, they get even *more* pleasure from this than we do—just because, I believe, they have a greater capacity for pleasure than we do. There is no reason to believe that this is a recent phenomenon. Wherever you go in the world, you see people interacting with dogs in this affectionate manner, and dogs returning the favor.

From the beginning, domestication could have been a two-way deal, with equality at its heart. It could have been mutual in that two species decided they liked each other and could get on. Basically, this is what happened with dogs (and probably with cats, too), and why we so often hear that dogs domesticated themselves—or even that dogs domesticated us. It was not, at its heart, an exploitative relationship. Dogs and cats were there not to be eaten but to be companions. For other animals, however, the point in domesticating them was to eat or exploit them. Could this have been otherwise?

Not so for other animals, starting about nine thousand years ago. The main animals domesticated from that point on were sheep (9000 B.C.E.), goats (9000 B.C.E.), cows (8000 B.C.E.), pigs (8000 B.C.E.), and chickens (2500 B.C.E.).[11] In *none* of these examples did we take into account the needs of the animal. Consider:

- They were there exclusively to be exploited. These were animals we wanted for *our* needs and we paid exactly zero attention to *their* needs. We didn't care what their life in the wild had been like, because we had no intention of attempting to replicate it in any way. Everything was done for our benefit, not theirs.

- A cow suckled her calf for a year in the wild, but we disrupted that cycle because we wanted the cow's milk for ourselves. Hens were no longer allowed to be with roosters, hatch their eggs and raise the chicks—we wanted the eggs for our consumption and we didn't care what the chickens wanted. Of course, early in the domestication process chickens had a much easier life; they were primarily kept for eggs, not for meat, and often had the run of the farm and even the house. Morally, however, we were still exploiting an animal for what it could give us, without considering what we could give to the animal. The same would apply to goats who were kept for their milk.

- Confinement was essential. Corrals, fences, cages, pens— anything to keep the animal from escaping, which, if you think about it, makes the idea that they chose to be there of their own accord ridiculous. Why would we need to stop them from leaving if they wanted to be there?

- Also, anything that gave them the power to escape had to be taken away, no matter how essential to their nature. We clipped their wings; we bred them to be so heavy they could barely move. We would not allow any interference in our pursuit of greed. More. More. More.

There is a terrible logic to animal suffering. As long as we believe we are entitled to their lives, we can do to them whatever increases our profit, *no matter how degrading or how much suffering or mutilation it causes them.*

Taking this even further, I believe that domestication was a bad deal *for us* as well:

- It coarsened us. It set a bad example for our children. How do you explain the Sixth Commandment, "Thou shalt not kill," to a child who recognizes that most of what she eats was once a living, feeling being?
- And what of the Eighth Commandment, "Do not steal"? What are we doing when we take milk, eggs, skin, and fur that do not belong to us?
- Our young children develop affection for an individual cow, sheep, or pig, and spend time caring for him or her. What do we say when the time comes to take the animal to the slaughterhouse? Modern apologists tell us that this is facing reality; it is introducing the child to the hard facts of life. But this is a reality of our making; the facts are hard because we made them so.

Dogs and cats are the exception. Yes, they may well have chosen domestication, but *no* other animal did, and no other animal except the human animal profits from it.

As with domestication, humans exploited other humans for their own ends, never for the sake of the people being exploited. Researchers on the history of slavery agree that it was modeled on the domestication of animals: although slavery goes back to prehistoric times, it does not antedate agriculture.

As late as 1919, a Portuguese delegate to the International Labor Conference in Geneva defended the exploitation of entire groups of people, saying, "The assimilation of the so-called inferior races, by cross-breeding, by means of the Christian religion, by the mixing of the most widely divergent elements; freedom of access to the highest offices of state, even in Europe—these are the principles which have always guided Portuguese colonization in Asia, in Africa, in the Pacific, and previously in America."[12]

Exploitation powered by greed is absent from other animal societies. Even fighting is different among animals. When top-ranking animal males fight for mating privileges, the consequences are rarely lethal. No apex predator sets out to get rid of all other apex predators. Moreover, those animals that get less than others do not seem to harbor resentment or spend their time thirsting and plotting vengeance, whereas human hunters killed off wolves almost to extinction because the wolves were their rivals for the deer and other game they wished to kill, and now are seen as a threat to domesticated livestock. Human greed is also destroying the natural world—even the oceans are being emptied of fish.

Is "surplus killing" in carnivores (wolves, coyotes, bears) in any way similar to this? It is a not very well understood phenomenon. We don't know how often it occurs in the wild, or under what circumstances. Generally, it has to do with wild animals coming upon fenced animals and not knowing what to make of the easy hunting. Wolves who have killed beyond what they need to eat immediately almost invariably take away the rest to bury. According to David Mech, the foremost authority on wolves, "surplus killing is rare and seems like surplus because they kill more than they can eat at the time. When we followed up on kills not all eaten right after being killed, the wolves eventually returned and ate them."[13]

Animal domestication has perpetuated a culture of cruelty and abuse. We watch animals who are our prisoners with no awareness of the suffering we have caused them. Are we ignorant or just indifferent? Might this help to explain what happens when humans watch other humans suffer and appear untroubled by their suffering?

9 · Indifference

The opposite of love is not hate, it's indifference.

—Elie Wiesel

WHEN THE ISRAELI KNESSET IN 1953 mandated the creation of a memorial to the victims of the Holocaust, Yad Vashem, one of their first tasks was to commemorate people they called "the Righteous Among the Nations." This term applies not to a particular nation but rather to non-Jewish individuals who, at risk to their own lives, saved Jews from extermination in various countries in Europe. Unlike the overwhelming majority of non-Jews in Europe and elsewhere, who thought, "This does not concern me"—in German, the phrase often heard was "Was geht das mich an?" (What is that to me?)—these people were not indifferent bystanders. In a culture of bystanders, they found themselves unable to simply stand by. They were the righteous when most others were not.

Sometimes people are slow to recognize evil or admit to themselves that someone is abusing others if the person seems polite. How many times have people said after a neighbor has committed a horrible act, "He seemed like such a nice guy"? Maybe they dress like us or resemble us in other ways we consider nonthreatening until their violent behavior is revealed.

Most of the time we are mere bystanders at the tragedy of others. Tragedies may occur a few feet away from us, as we are simply walking along a road, lost in our thoughts. If we were fully aware of all the misery going on around us, we surely would not be able to live at all. We would spend our entire life sobbing uncontrollably at the horror of it all.

Yet unless we become aware of the suffering around us, we risk losing our humanity. For the thought that others do not acknowledge our shared humanity is one of our greatest fears. This is similar to the fear that an animal views us as prey, but it is worse, because in the latter case we can understand; the former is a deep and horrible mystery. When we are suffering and others turn a blind eye to us and go on living in normal time, we may suddenly see ourselves in a different and frightening light; perhaps we even begin to doubt our own personal worth and humanity. People who emerge from prisons or from displaced-persons camps often speak of how disorienting it is to be in the ordinary world, a world in which they had no part and wonder if they ever will again. Must they not wonder how others could go on living their ordinary lives while they were tortured?

ALTHOUGH WE AVERT our eyes from suffering, there are situations in which we are more likely to get involved. When a hiker is missing, we volunteer to join a search party. When a person is drowning, we jump in. But in both these cases a person is in danger not from another person but from an impersonal force. This makes it easier to identify with the situation. When a person is assaulted or is otherwise the victim of violence, "This could happen to me" is not as readily apparent. This is especially true if the person is attacked because of his or her color or sexual preference and it is different from our own. Then we don't look for trouble: we mind our own business.

Whole nations sometimes respond to violence with indifference or a refusal to get involved. Many Americans were vehemently against entering the fighting during World War Two. I recently became aware of a letter that Thomas Mann sent to the American mythologist Joseph Campbell ("follow your bliss"), who was urging America to stay neutral in the war with Germany.

I always detested Joseph Campbell, long before reading an exposé in the *New York Review of Books* in which Brendan Gill reported on Campbell's anti-Semitism and his refusal to allow African Americans into his classes at Sarah Lawrence. Before the war, Campbell delivered a lecture, "Permanent Human Values," to students, urging them to stay away from politics. He made it clear he was opposed to America's entering the war on England's side. The lecture contained this inflammatory sentence, bound to enrage Thomas Mann: "We are all groping in this valley of tears, and if a Mr. Hitler collides with a Mr. Churchill, we are not in conscience bound to believe that a devil had collided with a saint." Mann wrote him a blistering response:

> It is curious, since you are a friend of my books, you must think that they have something to do with Permanent Human Values. Now these books are banned in Germany and in all the countries Germany at present dominates, and anyone who reads them, anyone who offers them for sale, anyone who even speaks well of me in public, would end in a concentration camp and his teeth would be knocked out, and his kidneys smashed. You maintain that we must not allow ourselves to be excited by this, we must rather see to the preservation of the lasting human values. That is strange.[2]

Mann had lived in Nazi Germany; he knew what he was talking about. To him, Campbell was a simple intellectual dilettante. He was aware, from direct experience, how dangerous it could be for neighbors to be indifferent to the suffering of others. He had experienced the burning of his own books.

Although sometimes when we note violence to others, we fear we could be next, there are times we fail to act for other reasons. Under what circumstances does being a bystander generate indifference?

Is it possible that some cultures reward indifference less than others and cultivate moral courage? I believe that in Italy and Denmark during the 1940s there was less of a tradition of indifference than in other cultures. This refusal to be a mere bystander helps explain why in Denmark more than 99 percent of the eight thousand Jews who lived there survived the war.[3] Yad Vashem gave the entire Danish resistance movement the title of Righteous Among the Nations. As for Italy, the Italian military was rarely willing to hand over Jews to their German allies because they knew they would be murdered. In late 1943, when Germany occupied Italy and demanded that Italian authorities hand over Jews for deportation, many non-Jewish Italians refused, including the Italian police.[4]

In Austria, by contrast, minding your own business in the 1930s was considered a civic virtue. The fate of their Jewish citizens was not uppermost in the minds of Austrians when Hitler "amalgamated" the two countries. Surprisingly, even neutral Switzerland and Sweden, where you would expect more resistance, copied Austria rather than Denmark or Italy.

An important literature exists about the refusal of countries such as England and the United States to help when they easily could have; it is painful to read. I recommend the novel by the Hungarian Austrian writer Hans Habe, *The Mission*, about the so-called attempt to save the Jews of Europe during a conference held in the French town of Évian-les-Bains in 1938, with representatives from thirty-two countries. Habe was himself present at the conference. What he makes clear is how profoundly unwilling all of the delegates were to do anything.

In most countries of Europe, the majority of people watched with something approaching indifference the destruction of their fellow citizens: Jews, Roma Sinti (known previously as Gypsies), the disabled, Jehovah's Witnesses, gay people, the so-called mentally ill, and of course political dissenters. Empathy and sympathy were in short supply.

IN THIS RESPECT, are we like other animals? It has struck many scientists—from Aristotle to Darwin and others—that an animal can observe another animal from his herd or flock taken by a predator with what appears to be almost complete indifference (though how we can be so certain is an interesting question).

Animal flocks, schools, shoals, herds, and packs clearly serve the function of safety in numbers, since a predator will have so many alternatives to choose from. But to believe this is the *only* purpose, as some biologists claim, is to omit the fact that these animals *like* to be together.[5] The urge to merge with a herd is a profound sensory and emotional need. Animals who do not have this urge, such as the big cats, pay a price in increased aggressiveness.

If after a traumatic event animals appear to continue on with their existence as if nothing life-altering had happened, this is not so different from our own reaction under similar circumstances. We make an exception, as do many other animals, when a member of one's family is endangered, especially a child.

But what prevents us from seeing *all* other humans as family? Is that completely unrealistic? Is indifference synonymous with apathy? This state of being without feeling for the external world, a form of dispassion, was for the Greeks (who called it *apatheia*) and even some Buddhists (whose *nishkāma* means, literally, "without love or desire") much to be desired. Even though I taught Sanskrit texts in which this achievement was praised, I never believed it possible or desirable. Slavoj Žižek in his recent book on violence remarks that the Buddhist solution to solidarity with every living being is "a universalized indifference—a learning of how to withdraw from too much empathy."[6] He claims that is why we see Zen Buddhism misused for a ruthless military attitude.[7] He has a point. We even see Buddhist fundamentalism (a term that seemed, in the past, almost an oxymoron) pressed into service in Sri Lanka to make the ridiculous claim that the Sinhalese are the original inhabitants of the island and the Tamils interlopers.

Like many people, I have a recurrent nightmare of being attacked while others observe without helping or intervening. Sartre cited Rimbaud: "Je est un autre" (I am an other). You can never be sure what the French mean by their aphorisms, but in this case I think Sartre meant that only to ourselves are we not other. Our nightmares reflect the fear and horror of being abandoned, alone, left to predators with no cover, no protection, and no backup. No wonder we cheer the superheroes in movies today: we would like to call on them when in danger. Surely part of the attraction for any child living with a dog is the recognition that the dog will protect the child in case of any attack, with no thought to her own safety. As far as she is concerned, the child comes first.

I have earlier claimed that no wild animal helps a member of another species as consistently as do humans. Dogs are an exception, but they are not a wild species, and have been domesticated for so long that we can almost regard them as a member of our own species, as many people do ("My dog is part of my family," many of us say, and mean it). There are occasional reports of dolphins rescuing humans, but it is extremely rare for any nonhuman except dogs to come to the rescue of another species while endangering his or her own life.

When we see something terrible happen to a neighbor, at the least there *must* be an unconscious identification: "It could have been me." Perhaps our seeming indifference is really a mask for fear: "If I intervene, something violent will happen to me as well?" In some countries (such as Argentina, Israel, Australia, and Canada) it is even illegal to stand by if somebody else is in danger without attempting to help. The paradigm case is that of Kitty Genovese.

In New York City on March 13, 1964, Kitty Genovese was stabbed to death by a stranger. The *New York Times* published a short notice the next day, but when Abe Rosenthal, then the paper's metropolitan editor, met with Michael J. Murphy, the police commissioner at the time, and heard the full story, he commissioned an article to run on the front page. Entitled "Thirty Eight Who Saw Murder Didn't Call the Police," by Martin Gansberg, the piece opened with this statement: "For more than half an hour 38 respectable, law-abiding citizens in Queens watched a killer stalk and stab a woman in three separate attacks in Kew Gardens."[8] Rosenthal later that year published a book about the incident, *Thirty Eight Witnesses: The Kitty Genovese Case.*[9]

The lack of response by her neighbors became the focus of much research in the field of social psychology into what became known as the "bystander effect." The story of the "witnesses who did nothing" is taught in every introductory psychology class in the United States and Britain, and in many other countries. It is thought that the passive bystanders were under the influence of "pluralistic ignorance"—defined as the tendency to mistake the calm demeanor of other people present as a sign that no emergency is actually taking place. It is true that several people claimed they thought the assault was merely a lovers' quarrel, yet when she was stabbed, Kitty yelled out: "Oh my God, he stabbed me! Help me! Please help me!" Who could mistake that for a mere difference of opinion? And when she was attacked and stabbed a second time minutes later, she yelled: "I'm dying! I'm dying!"[10]

Nowhere was the case more affecting than among America's psychologists. "It was monumental," said Harold Takooshian, a professor of urban psychology at Fordham University. Before the murder, he added, "nobody really had any idea why people did not help, and conversely why people did help. The psychologists were really stunned by their lack of information on this."[11]

It has also been pointed out that all of the many commentators missed the misogyny that was part of the killing. This is given further credence when we reflect that Kitty was lesbian, living in the apartment with her partner, Mary Ann Zielonko, and this fact was not even mentioned in the article. Zielonko is quoted (by Jim Rasenberger) as saying: "We were lovers together. Everybody tried to hush that up."[12]

Much has been made of the claim that the facts as reported in the original article were not completely accurate: the *Times* article spoke of three attacks by the man when in fact there were only two; it mentioned thirty-eight witnesses, but the number appears to have been fewer; nobody phoned the police, the article said, but probably two people did. These errors have been pointed out a number of times, most notably by a maritime lawyer named Joseph de May Jr.[13] While de May was able to correct a number of errors, including how many people "witnessed" the crime, it is important to note that the assistant district attorney responsible for the case had this to say: "I don't think 38 people witnessed it . . . I don't know where that came from, the 38. I didn't count 38. We only found half a dozen that saw what was going on, that we could use." Half a dozen is still a lot of people, and the meaning is clear: they *saw* what happened. But many more *heard* what happened, according to the police commissioner: "I believe that many people heard the screams," he said. "It could have been more than 38. And anyone that heard the screams had to know there was a vicious crime taking place. There's no doubt in my mind about that."[14]

Moreover, people acknowledged that they were reluctant to help. One man explained that he had called the police after much deliberation. He had phoned a friend in Nassau County for advice and then had crossed the roof of the building to the apartment of an elderly woman to get her to make the call. "I didn't want to get involved," he sheepishly told police. Another witness, "a distraught woman, wiping her hands on her apron, said, 'I didn't want my husband to get involved.'" A third, when asked why she hadn't called the police, "shrugged and replied: 'I don't know.'" Far worse is the final response: "A man peeked out from a slight opening in the doorway to his apartment and rattled off an account of the killer's second attack. Why hadn't he called the police at the time? 'I was tired,' he said without emotion. 'I went back to bed.'"

Surely, then, the point of the original article is intact and is not something that can be dismissed as a total anomaly. Nor is this a unique example of the phenomenon under question.

IN 2010, A homeless man named Hugo Alfredo Tale-Yax, a Guatemalan immigrant, tried to stop a violent mugging in Queens, New York, by defending the woman being assaulted and robbed. The assailant stabbed Tale-Yax and ran. Tale-Yax fell bleeding onto the sidewalk. From the time-lapse video of a nearby surveillance camera we learn that over the course of more than an hour, almost twenty-five people walked right past Tale-Yax without doing anything to help him. Several people stopped and stared at the man bleeding to death on the sidewalk but did nothing. One man turned him over, saw the blood pooling beneath him, and left. Another man came out of a nearby building, took a picture of Tale-Yax with his cell phone, and left. Even the woman Tale-Yax saved from the robbery failed to call the police. Most simply looked at him with mild curiosity, and hurried on. Finally someone dialed 911. When firefighters arrived an hour and twenty minutes after the stabbing, Tale-Yax, just thirty-one years old, was dead. When asked by a reporter for the *New York Times* a few days later, most said that they had not wanted to get involved, or just wanted to mind their own business. There is no legal obligation in New York State to help a person in dire distress.[15]

The explanations offered by psychiatrists and psychologists are often unhelpful. "According to Washington psychiatrist Dr. Alen Salerian [who had been head of the FBI's Mobile Psychiatric Emergency Response team], humans are hardwired in the deepest recesses of the brain to avoid involvement. 'In many ways, it repeats animal behavior that most animals when they see danger they stay away from it.'"

WHATEVER THE PARTICULARS of the Kitty Genovese story, I find it odd that psychologists repeatedly attempt to replicate some version of this horrible crime in a laboratory. Stanley Milgram's experiments on obedience to authority figures (not to mention the earlier deprivation experiments on monkeys by Harry Harlow), Martin Seligman's learned-helplessness experiments on dogs, and Phil Zimbardo's prison experiment on Stanford undergraduates were not only cruel and/or ethically questionable but also unnecessary.[16]

In each and every case, we learn more from addressing the questions in real time in the real world. Harry Harlow could easily see what happened to babies who were deprived of their mothers at an early age by visiting institutions. René Spitz did just this in his famous studies of children who died of neglect in homes in

Switzerland right after the Second World War.[17] Stanley Milgram was far more likely to learn about obedience to authority figures by looking at accounts of what happened during the war (which is what gave rise to the experiments in the first place).[18] Phil Zimbardo lived close to San Quentin and could learn all he needed about prisons and inmates right on his doorstep. Martin Seligman, who applied his "research" to depressed people and women who were living in abusive relationships, could just as easily have talked to those people as torture dogs.[19]

Reading, studying, and observing, without trying to re-create ugly situations, are far more likely to yield insight into human nature than a contrived experiment where one can never know how aware of the situation any so-called naive subject really is. Many of those studied by Milgram, who "shocked" an actor who was hired to pretend to be the subject of the experiment and to behave as if he really were being shocked when in fact he was not, knew or strongly suspected that the whole experiment was a setup, a sham—which is why they played along. Milgram does not mention this possibility. It is too easy to claim, as Milgram did, that we are all, at best, potential torturers. This leaves real torturers off the hook: they are, according to Milgram, doing what the rest of us could just as easily have done, given slightly altered circumstances. It also does not account for the substantial number of people who actually refused to shock others.

In fact, the motivation of researchers such as Latane and Darley, who were the first to write about the bystander phenomenon (using Kitty Genovese as their main example), seems to be to redeem those accused of immoral or unfeeling behavior, which they call "collective inaction." But they had a major war (or two) behind them already, and could examine eyewitness accounts of the inaction of citizens during the war when other fellow citizens were being persecuted. Surely understanding the bystander phenomenon when it really counted and in real time was more important than artificial experiments at a university. Why should it take experiments with undergraduates to understand puzzling features of a recent war?

It is a good tendency to think of indifference as bad. Humans are *supposed* to care, and when they don't, we see something amiss. When I visit my ninety-five-year-old mother, I expect to see the indifference that I encounter in her home, because I know that it is one of the clinical signs of Alzheimer's disease.[20] I still find it upsetting, in spite of what I know. Similarly, we don't criticize the Bolshevik virtue of *tverdost*, "hardness," which refers to the indifference Russians felt or appeared to feel for those who disappeared into the gulags; anyone displaying anything else at the time might have wound up accompanying them. But strategic indifference is not what we are addressing here.

FOR A GOOD part of our history, humans were prey to larger predators. Not "man the hunter," but "man the hunted," as a new and excellent book is titled.[21] We don't like to think of ourselves as mere cat food, but when you think of how delicate we are in our bodies compared to the other apex predators, it becomes clear that without modern weapons, we had to be a fearful, timid species, much like a deer. We are not big cats; we don't have their insouciance. We have fingers, not claws; our small jaws have teeth designed to eat, not hunt; our arms are not suited to climbing into trees to make a safe getaway, nor are they powerful enough to fight back if attacked. We had to rely on cunning, avoidance, fire, hiding, and language to alert others to dangers lurking nearby. The terror of predation is still with us. We are fascinated and repulsed by stories of humans who are attacked by sharks, crocodiles, or any other animal predator.

As Paul Trout has explained in his book *Deadly Powers: Animal*

Predators and the Mythic Imagination, early humans when confronted with skulls and bones of huge animals had no way of knowing these carnivorous "monsters" were long extinct. So their "hyper predator detection system . . . would have prompted them to interpret the bones as the remains of creatures still alive and possibly lurking somewhere in the environment." We see monsters everywhere.

In spite of this, I think our response to human predation by other humans is still like that of many other animals, a form of indifference. Dawkins frightened us when he wrote, "The universe we observe has precisely the properties we should expect if there is, at bottom, no design, no purpose, no evil and no good, nothing but blind, pitiless indifference." Keep in mind the bon mot of François de La Rochefoucauld, the cynical observer of Louis XIV's court, when he said, "Man has an infinite capacity for enduring the suffering of others." If those "others" are animals, the path to encouraging empathy is a steep one indeed.

We are understandably amazed and (some of us) delighted when we learn of people who, in the middle of a human catastrophe—Hurricane Katrina, for example—take time and energy to consider the plight of animals left behind. During World War Two Antonina Zabinski (the wife of the director of the Warsaw Zoo, who, with her husband, was made a Righteous Among the Nations by Yad Vashem after the war) saw the German SS shooting the animals at the Warsaw zoo, and wrote in her diary with great perception: "How many humans will die like this in the coming months?" She saw how the two phenomena were linked. When we ignore suffering, whether animal or human, are we then reverting to an ancient legacy from our two-million-year history, one in keeping with the indifference of other animals?

Just as animals try not to be noticed as a way of protecting themselves, the same is true for humans as well. As a teenager I was traveling by myself on a train in Argentina when I noticed a dangerous-looking man scanning the passengers. I willed myself not to look at him but I could not help myself, and I stared a second too long. He caught my glance, came over, and menacingly asked me why I was looking at him. He got louder and more aggressive, but fortunately it was a crowded train, people told him to keep quiet, and he did, while continuing to glare at me. I took the first opportunity to leave the train. At that moment, I felt I had escaped predation.

From our vantage point, indifference appears to be widespread in the animal world, but in truth we don't know what other animals in the herd feel when a predator claims one of its members. What we see as indifference may well be something we do not recognize, or for which we have no word or understanding. It is hard enough to understand human feelings. Even Darwin acknowledged that when a cow looks at a dead herd mate, we couldn't possibly know what goes through her mind.

The major difference in the natural world is that wild animals do not have to deal with psychopathy, unless we ourselves have created artificial traumas.[22] They do not have to watch as one of their own is bullied or tortured or murdered for no reason. They are used to understanding the reason that a familiar animal is taken by a predator: it is for food. This in no way mimics human bullying or human sociopathy. (I use *psychopathy* when there is a criminal element and *sociopathy* for the more common kind of cold lack of feeling.) Sociopaths, we say, have no feelings of sympathy, or empathy. If they are the source of pain, they feel no remorse or, worse, take pleasure in the suffering they have created. Animals do not have to worry about sociopaths the way we do. Not only do humans fear such people nowadays, but we fear they are becoming less visible and more widespread; hence books such as *Snakes in Suits: When Psychopaths Go to Work*.

Cute title, but in reality there is no such thing as a psychopathic snake. Snakes are simply doing what snakes do. They have no personal stake in the matter. Only humans can be psychopaths. Only humans create drone aircraft that kill from a distance, impersonally. Michael Moore says: "Now we send in remote pilotless planes to kill, planes that are being controlled by faceless men in a lush, air conditioned studio in suburban Las Vegas. It is madness."

In this case, the madness is not a psychiatric condition, but something fundamentally flawed in the human heart. In *Snakes in Suits*, the authors write of a primitive, autonomic, and fearful response to a predator. They describe the psychopath as an intraspecies predator.[23] We, the victims, fear other humans behaving like predators, for we do not want to be prey. In the 2012 movie *Chronicle*, when the superhero boy with magic powers "goes to the dark side," he yells: "I am the apex predator!"

Maybe indifference is at its root defensive, a reaction to fear, the fear of annihilation. The problem is that once it becomes a way of life, it invades more and more of our emotional lives.

But when I point to the ubiquity of indifference in the natural world, I am not suggesting that no animal ever comes to the aid of another in an altruistic act. Quite the contrary. More and more scientists have given convincing evidence of how prevalent such compassion is. We find it even in rats and mice. What is rarer is to witness an animal rescue another animal from a different species. But while rare, it does happen, and in my book *When Elephants Weep* I gave several examples. They could be multiplied today. (Also, we should note that they may well happen with no human present to witness them.) Nonetheless, animals are not designed to risk their lives for animals of a different species. We are not either, but we do it nonetheless. This lovely puzzle is at the heart of the altruism paradox.

Dale Peterson, in his book *The Moral Lives of Animals*, mentions the case of a young African forest elephant who had collapsed off to one side of a narrow, sandy trail in a Central African forest. On this distressing day, thirty-eight elephants made fifty-six visits to her. Several elephants seemed to want to assist the dying elephant, attempting to push or lift her upright, even though these elephants were not related to her. Peterson notes, "These apparent acts of kindness, then, might be examples of true altruism."

In another example cited in the book, an elephant matriarch charged a Kenyan ranch worker, knocked him down, and broke his leg. The next day trackers found him propped up against a tree but defended by a large elephant. He stopped them from shooting the elephant, explaining that this was the same elephant who had attacked him, but (feeling remorse or guilt?) she had used her trunk to pull him over to the tree where there was shade, and gently pulled him upright with her foot. Her family moved on, but she stayed with him for the rest of the day and the entire night, continually touching him with her trunk to comfort him. She also chased away a herd of wild buffalo who might have come too close. "The injured man believed that the elephant had deliberately tried to care for and protect him."[24]

Frans de Waal, in his wonderful book *The Age of Empathy*, tells the strange story of Ahla, a baboon "employed" by a goat farmer in Africa. She had a mania for putting mothers and offspring together: the minute a kid bleated and asked for her mother, Ahla would carry her under her arm to the next barn, where the mothers were kept, and shove her underneath the correct mother for nursing. She never made a mistake! Was she displaying annoyance at the noise, remarkable training, or simple altruism?

De Waal also describes an old bull elephant who walked to a spring to bring water to a dying companion, spraying it over the other bull's head and ears and attempting to get him to drink. He saw the problem and tried in his own way to fix it.

Of course we can find hundreds of such examples in human societies, enough to fill a large encyclopedia. But—and this is de Waal's point—until recently such examples were considered near impossible in animal societies but for the very occasional anecdote, which scientists dismissed as just that.

The English philosopher Mary Midgley was among the first to point out that philosophers such as Plato, Aristotle, and Kant considered animals not as *symbols* of evil but as evil in and of themselves.[25] With this pedigree, no wonder it is taking us so long to remove ourselves from the tentacles of false beliefs.

Humans are rarely sentimental (that is, have feelings) about what they eat and how what they eat came to be food. I am sure animals, too, are rarely, if ever, sentimental about a meal. Perhaps the roots of indifference are to be found in our willingness to eat what was once a living, feeling animal. If we gave that up, would we reconnect with feelings we have suppressed, repressed, or never known?

10 · Wolves

The wolf exerts a powerful influence on the human imagination.
It takes your stare and turns it back on you.

—Barry Lopez, *Of Wolves and Men*

 IN MANY WAYS, WOLVES DO NOT fit the pattern I have been examining in this book. In North America they are no threat to humans at all. They are far more likely to run from an encounter with a human than attack, even when in a pack and the human is solitary (as all wolf biologists will confirm). But this is not a universal characteristic of wolves. In India and Russia they appear to behave differently. Like so many others, including the Nobel Prize winner Konrad Lorenz, I believed that wolves almost never killed other wolves.

However, recent research by David Mech, arguably the world's leading authority on wolves, claims that wolf mortality is primarily due to wolf-on-wolf aggression. Mech writes to me that I should consider 25 percent of all wolf fatalities as due to other wolves! I am sure he knows whereof he writes, but he left out of this statistic something that is coming into focus only recently, mostly as a result of the work Gay Bradshaw has done with elephants.

Anomalous behavior—hyperaggressivity, for example—can be partially or fully explained when one considers human induced stress and trauma. (This is somewhat similar to Jane Goodall linking chimpanzee aggression to humans feeding bananas to chimps; see chapter 5.) Bradshaw writes convincingly of adolescent elephants who suffer the equivalent of human post-traumatic stress disorder. PTSD is *not* part of the natural world of elephants. (Is it even part of our natural world?) It did not exist until we arrived on the scene to cause elephants and other animals to veer from their natural pathways, both literally and figuratively. I asked Bradshaw to clarify her position in terms of animals besides elephants. She wrote me:

> Our entire Western culture, what we call civilization, is traumatogenic, meaning it creates conditions which make trauma possible or even likely. Elephants, parrots, the great apes, and others, have been reliably diagnosed with PTSD. But all other wildlife is also likely beset with trauma-related conditions given what they have been subjected to: successive mass killings, habitat destruction and fragmentation, torture (traps, for example), all of which can lead to social breakdown (something we see even on farms, when animals behave in aggressive ways *because* of what we do to them, which we then attribute to their very nature). Our entire cultural pattern of interpretation is violent. We see violence because that is what we are looking for. Wolves are no more violent than an elephant before the series of broad scale genocides and *Anschluss* (the appropriation of nature—wildlife, land, and lives), starting with agriculture that permitted and enabled large-scale killing and environmental destruction.

Why wouldn't the effects of trauma take their toll on wolves as well? Only in the last ten thousand years have we been hunting wolves—that is, only since agriculture and domestication.

Native Americans hunted wolves, but sparingly (primarily, I believe, to use their warm fur for winter clothing). Many tribes never hunted them, regarding them as their totem animal or even as their ancestor—in any event, as sacred. Wolves were highly respected by native cultures everywhere, both as great hunters and as a highly sociable species with special family bonds not unlike our own. They called them "pathfinders." But once Europeans colonized North America, relations with wolves changed drastically, especially when there were stock animals to protect from predators like them. We saw wolves as the enemy, as a competitor. We were raising animals for food and wolves wanted the same food. We hunted them, putting bounties on their head, and humans committed themselves to the wolves' extermination. How could this not affect wolves' behavior, not only toward us but also toward one another? A trauma is by definition an event that is unexpected, one that is bound to confuse and disorganize the psyche.

It may well be that our entire species has suffered a kind of PTSD since the origins of agriculture and domestication of animals, as I have argued throughout this book (a point made first, I believe, by Jim Mason, but also by Will Tuttle in his book *The World Peace Diet*). If we accept this, then we have a great deal in common with other animals and *their* traumatisms, the difference being that we are responsible for theirs *and* for ours and they are responsible for neither.

WOLVES OCCUPY A special place in the Western psyche. They are clearly the ancestors of our beloved dogs, and pretty much the entire Western world loves dogs, to judge by the number of people who live with them: 40 percent of American households. Hence the outrage when Sarah Palin cheerfully announced that she chased wolves from planes until they collapsed from exhaustion, then shot them. Palin urged others to do the same, despite the fact that Alaskans themselves had voted against aerial shooting in 2000.

However, we also use wolves as a metaphor for all the horrors of which a man is capable. Hence the often-invoked ancient Latin phrase *Homo homini lupus*, "Man is a wolf to [his fellow] man." Just as wolves prey on wolves, so man preys on man.[1] It is questionable whether wolves prey on other wolves. For a long time, most wolf biologists believed that in fact they do not. (I say believed in the past tense because there seems to be a shift recently.) You certainly would believe they prey on man if you were raised with Little Red Riding Hood, the Boy Who Cried Wolf, the Big Bad Wolf, Peter and the Wolf, *The Chronicles of Narnia*, and other fantasy tales of this nature. Then you very well might see "the wolf at the door."

In Joe Carnahan's 2011 film *The Grey* with Liam Neeson, a group of men who survive a plane crash in the Alaskan wilderness are preyed upon by enormous, vicious wolves with only one thing on their mind: killing out of vengeance and hatred. The wolves pick off the men one by one. Many commentators were highly indignant that the wolves in this film were portrayed as evil, just as in medieval times. A number of biologists weighed in, all correcting this faulty portrayal of the wolves, which had not a shred of truth in it.

In fact, there have been only two documented cases of a wolf actually killing a human in the history of North America. In 2005, in an incident still under investigation, Kenton Carnegie, a twenty-two-year-old geology student, was apparently attacked and killed by four wolves while hiking in remote northern Saskatchewan. In March 2010, thirty-two-year-old Candice Berner, a special education teacher, was set on by at least two wolves while out for a late afternoon jog on a road outside Chignik Lake, a fishing village on the Alaska Peninsula, about 475 miles southwest of Anchorage.

When Europeans arrived in the New World, roughly 250,000 wolves flourished in what are now the lower forty-eight states. Altogether in North America, there must have been between one and two million wolves. In 1630, just ten years after the *Mayflower* landed at Plymouth Rock, the Massachusetts Bay Colony began offering a bounty for every wolf killed. In a twenty-five-year-period at the turn of the twentieth century, more than eighty thousand wolves were killed in Montana alone. The war against the wolf began early, and the persecution has continued more or less until the present day. By the 1970s, only five hundred to a thousand wolves remained in the lower forty-eight states, on less than 3 percent of their former range. Both the Mexican gray wolf and the red wolf were completely eliminated in the wild, although there have been recent reintroduction efforts. Gray wolves in the lower forty-eight states now number about twenty-six hundred. The belief that wolves pose a deadly threat to human safety has persisted despite every attempt to document the contrary. Education is no match for deeply ingrained stereotypes known from childhood.

Wolves have been completely exterminated in many other places around the world. Sir Ewan Cameron killed the last Scottish wolf in 1680. In Ireland, the last wolf died in 1786. In France from 1818 to 1829, fourteen thousand wolves were killed each year. At the end of the First World War, the population was estimated to be between 150 and 200 animals. The last confirmed French wolf kill occurred in 1937. In the seventeenth century, the Swedish king Magnus Eriksson declared wolf hunting a civic duty, with only priests and landless women exempted. Somebody killed Sweden's last wolf in 1966, after which the species was declared legally protected. In Norway, the last wolf was killed in 1976.[2]

WHEN WE SPEAK of a wolf as a "bloodthirsty beast," we are engaging in pure anthropomorphism. A pack of wolves cannot be said to be vicious when there is a productive endpoint to their behavior.

Sometimes when my ninety-pound golden Labrador retriever, Benjy, is resting on the bed, I will lift up his lips to show my two boys his large canine teeth and powerful jaws. "Awesome," they say, with respect. He descended from a powerful predator. An apex predator. No animal in the wild attacks such an animal. He stands atop the food chain. This aggression has been completely bred out of Benjy. Most dogs find it difficult to resist chasing a squirrel, whereas Benjy wants to lick them. He poses no threat to our resident rats, or the three cats, or the birds on the beach. Indeed, Benjy was recently found to be communing with a lovely green praying mantis. Like a child, he comes to me when he is hurt. He shows me his paw and whines. He expects me to remove whatever is bothering him, and of course I do. He trusts me—again, just like my own child—to help him when he needs me. This enchants me. But in this behavior, he is no longer a wolf. However, while playing on the beach, Benjy reverts, briefly, to a supreme predator: he grabs a stick and dares me to take it away. He growls menacingly, but his tail is going a mile a minute. He is playing, he is joking, and he knows it, and he knows I know it, too. In this game, he becomes the big bad wolf and I the helpless small human. He runs circles around me, dares me to try to catch him. In this incarnation, it would take a dozen men to subdue him. He is my physical superior; of that there can be no doubt.

Humans are intrigued by the question of whether wolves ever hunt humans in the way that we hunt wolves. I suppose people are wondering about payback, just as in the movie *The Grey*. But wolves, at least today, do not hunt humans in North America. Wolf biologists rarely even see a wolf. Wolves rarely attack humans. Why they don't is a different question. Douglas Smith, the leader of the

Yellowstone Wolf Project in Yellowstone National Park, writes to me that there were no attacks by wolves on humans from 1995, when they were first introduced to the park, until 2009 (when a study was completed).[3] This fact does not prevent some people from falsely viewing wolves as the ultimate predator of humans, a belief perhaps rooted in our evolutionary history when we would have been far more vulnerable to wolf attacks.[4] In Norway, where apparently a wolf has neither killed nor injured anybody for the past two hundred years and where wolves have been extinct since 1976, half of the entire population responded to a recent questionnaire saying that they are "very much afraid of wolves."[5]

I wonder whether wolves have learned to avoid humans in North America precisely because we hunted them nearly to extinction. Is it not the case that *all* animals we have hunted aggressively fear and avoid us—whales, the big cats, bears? We have to assume they recognize what has happened and are able to convey to their young that humans represent a special threat.

I am not attempting to whitewash or romanticize wolves, suggesting they feel a kinship with us based on the shared traits of group hunting, cooperation, altruism toward young, sociability, and so on. That would be to make a lot of assumptions. Moreover, it leaves unexplained the fact that wolves are a real danger in other parts of the world. In India, for example, several hundred children appear to have been killed by wolves. In eastern Uttar-Pradesh in 1996, a single wolf was found to be responsible for attacks on seventy-six children, all under the age of ten. Fifty of these attacks were fatal. The reasons for the high number of (mostly) children killed in India are not entirely clear, and it is possible that it has little to do with natural wolf behavior. In most of the cases investigated, the wolves were stressed by a lack of natural prey; children are three times as likely to be unescorted as livestock; and the wolves are habituated to humans. It is not always easy to understand what happens between humans and animals in India and accurate information is not easy to come by. That said, I agree with wolf researcher Bruce Weide, who notes: "We do wolves a disservice if we strive to mold them into saints of the wild . . . Wolves don't care if they're your totem animal."[6]

Russia is another special case. This is where most accounts of wolf attacks on defenseless humans in sleds originate. Many of the accounts are meant to be fiction, or are fantasies influenced by fiction—children on a troika attacked by wolves is a staple of Russian literature. As is the case with India, the information we have about such attacks is not always reliable. We cannot say how many humans wolves in Russia have killed over the last hundred years, but we do know that from 1950 until 1954, Russians killed an average of 50,000 wolves annually. If we wish, however, to explain wolf attacks on humans in Russia based on human hunting of wolves, we are faced with the paradox that wolves responded to gun attacks in North America by making themselves almost invisible and never attacking humans, whereas in Russia they behaved in the opposite manner. What could account for this disparity remains a mystery.

THE JAPANESE EARLY in their history respected the wolf as Oguchi no Magami, or Large-Mouthed Pure God, but this goodwill did not last. In the eighteenth century, wolves were seen as rabid man-killers in many parts of Japan, though there is no historical evidence they ever were. I have never been a fan of the word *demonize*, but in this case it was literally true: wolves were thought of as demons. The Japanese organized highly ritualized hunts to cleanse the landscape of wolves. The ritual was no doubt thought necessary to ward off the magic powers they had invested in wolves. By the nineteenth century it was simply slaughter, similar to what happened in the

United States during the same period, including the use of poisons that brought on prolonged and incredible suffering. This sadistic exercise tells us more about humans than it does about wolves. We learn from Brett Walker's fine book that Japanese wolf scientists still camp out in the hopes of hearing a wolf. But they experience only quiet. This is a warning to us of the profound silence that awaits all humanity when, as the Japanese priest Kenko taught almost seven centuries ago, we "look on fellow sentient creatures without feeling compassion."

We have almost entirely eradicated the world's population of wolves, millions of them, because we have falsely believed they were our enemies, bent on harming us. The truth is much different. If any wild animal has ever been the ideal candidate to be our bosom friend, it is the wolf. But while the idea of a dog as a human's best friend represents the truth, even a cliché, the far more deadly concept of the wolf as a vicious killer is deeply entrenched in the human psyche, much to the detriment of one of the most noble of all beasts.

There can be no doubt that early in our species's history we tamed wolves and recognized their capacity for a deep friendship with us based on mutual affection. While we retained this knowledge and these feelings for dogs, we lost them when it came to wolves, a loss with profound repercussions for wolves and also for us. We traumatized wolves; we may also in the process have traumatized ourselves, numbing or losing something of our natural ability and inclination to feel sympathy and compassion.

EVER SINCE I wrote *Dogs Never Lie About Love*, and in several books about animals since, I have contended that wolves are not suitable as companions (known in the past as "pets"). They are not domesticated animals, I wrote, and no matter how tame, one never knew when they might revert to their nature as a wild animal. Would I allow my young children to play with such an animal? Not likely.

Then a short time ago, while in Los Angeles with friends, I ran into Lorin Lindner, a Ph.D. psychologist who many years ago started a parrot sanctuary (www.parrotcare.org) still thriving on twenty acres of garden on the grounds of the Department of Veterans Affairs West Los Angeles Medical Center, where returning veterans get to work with therapists with feathers. Lorin and her husband, Matthew, now run a wolf sanctuary in the hills about an hour north of Los Angeles called Lockwood Animal Rescue Center. My sons, Manu, twelve, and Ilan, seventeen, were immediately alert: "Dad, please can we go?" So before returning to Auckland, we stopped at the sanctuary. We had only a few hours, but I have to say it was among the most amazing two hours I have ever spent, and my family would concur. As soon as we got out of the car, six dogs surrounded us, and without further ado we were ushered into the large wolf enclosure, where Manu was immediately the object of affectionate attention. Wolves were licking his face; others rubbed against him like cats; still others wanted to play. Ilan and Manu were transported into wolf heaven.

Before I could register a single objection, or even attempt to give voice to my (apparently mistaken) views on how dangerous wolves could be, Lorin and Mathew and the two boys were playing and laughing and running around with wolves of all kinds. "Low-content wolves" (the new politically correct term I learned from Lorin), "medium-content wolves," "high-content wolves," and pure wolves were all as playful, as friendly, and as eager to please as any dog I have ever known. We walked over to the house, and there, on the balcony, were another eight wolves. They had two acres to play in, but they were all eagerly awaiting us, tails wagging, chuffing with delighted anticipation. They wanted to be around humans!

These were all wolves who had been rescued. One had even been shot by a human but found it in her heart to forgive. Others had been abandoned or had become too wild to keep. But with the constant love that Lorin gives them, they have become completely accustomed to humans. More than that: they *want* to be around humans. Though a wolf can be individually traumatized, even shot at and wounded, he can forgive, following the old but lovely cliché that to forgive is canine. Could the same be true for us? I hope so, and that is why I investigate the nature of kindness in the next chapter.

11 · Kindness?

You cannot do a kindness too soon, for you never know how soon it will be too late.

—Ralph Waldo Emerson

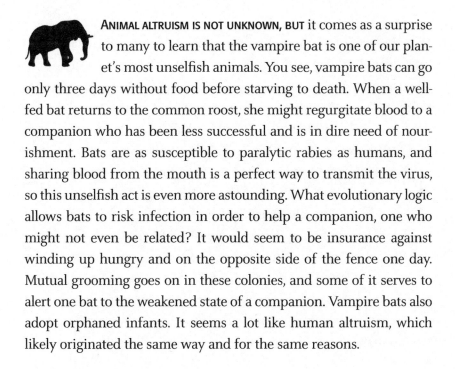 ANIMAL ALTRUISM IS NOT UNKNOWN, BUT it comes as a surprise to many to learn that the vampire bat is one of our planet's most unselfish animals. You see, vampire bats can go only three days without food before starving to death. When a well-fed bat returns to the common roost, she might regurgitate blood to a companion who has been less successful and is in dire need of nourishment. Bats are as susceptible to paralytic rabies as humans, and sharing blood from the mouth is a perfect way to transmit the virus, so this unselfish act is even more astounding. What evolutionary logic allows bats to risk infection in order to help a companion, one who might not even be related? It would seem to be insurance against winding up hungry and on the opposite side of the fence one day. Mutual grooming goes on in these colonies, and some of it serves to alert one bat to the weakened state of a companion. Vampire bats also adopt orphaned infants. It seems a lot like human altruism, which likely originated the same way and for the same reasons.

Bats are among the animal world's best mothers. They birth pups weighing as much as 40 percent of the mother's body weight (imagine if human babies weighed seventy pounds at birth!) and nurse them for more than six months—a long time for such a small mammal. Mothers also nurse unrelated pups. It was thought for some time that they could not tell who their own babies were, but they know perfectly well. It is presumed that they do this so that their own babies benefit from similar benevolence on the part of a different but equally unrelated mother. Some females have been seen helping to groom baby bats not their own, and sometimes even helping maneuver them into the proper suckling position. Young vampire bats show no aggressive behavior when they play and wrestle with other juveniles. In the roost, juveniles perform a gesture of appeasement by lifting a folded wing, as if to say, "I mean no harm."

NOW THAT WE have at last shed the image of the gorilla as a natural killer, people today will not be surprised to learn of the role that altruism plays in gorilla society. Gorillas can live for forty years or more. Scientists studying them, contrary to expectations, discovered that when gorillas grow too old to look after themselves, other gorillas provide them with care. Gorillas will also treat other sick gorillas who can no longer keep up with the rest of the troupe by giving them special herbs they find in the jungle to help cure them of their illness. The silverback male will sometimes adopt a baby if she is orphaned, taking care of her and protecting her, even allowing the infant to share his nest at night. He shows extraordinary patience, tolerance, and obvious affection. Naturalists studying gorillas in the wild have seen young gorillas play with a large silverback or wrestle with one another on top of the adult gorilla's body. No one has ever seen a silverback or an adult female hit a young gorilla in anger. In fact, gorillas always avoid fights with other animals, even when those animals are considerably weaker. Gorillas make a lot of noise but rarely attack, in spite of the male's huge canine teeth.

We have seen that when it comes to complex, deep, almost unimaginable violence, our species is beyond compare. By our species, of course, I don't mean every person in the entire species. However, among us there are individuals—*many* of them—who commit this violence. This is not the case with other species. When it comes to the opposite, altruism, we also have the same very large spread: there are those who are minimally altruistic (some not at all) and then there are those who truly go the whole distance, people who are household names or ought to be. These include Raoul Wallenberg, the Swedish diplomat in Budapest who saved thousands of Hungarian Jews from certain death, and the young people in the White Rose in Munich who were beheaded for their active resistance to Hitler. Many would name Nelson Mandela of South Africa; the Mothers of the Plaza de Mayo, who stood up to the Argentine junta; Oskar Schindler (of *Schindler's List* fame); Mahatma Gandhi; Rosa Parks; Chiune Sugihara, the Japanese vice consul in Lithuania who issued thousands of transit visas to Jews, thereby saving their lives, at great risk to his own life. We admire Paul Rusesabagina, the manager of the Hotel des Mille Collines in Kigali, who saved 1,268 Tutsis and Hutus during the 1994 Rwandan genocide (as dramatized in the fine 2004 film *Hotel Rwanda*). Rusesabagina was not related to any of these people and was in considerable danger of losing his life, yet he persisted.

Many of us are deeply concerned with people who are not relatives, or even with creatures who are not even people. That we can care about another species is quite astonishing. Consider a fairly typical example: Recently, more than 150 public-interest organizations representing millions of Americans called on the Obama administration to "give polar bears the protection they need and deserve under the law." Many of these people will never have any direct interaction with polar bears, yet they care about this living being, even if they never expect to see one. People make fun of those who care about the conservation of the spotted owl and the small fish known as the snail darter from eastern Tennessee. I find it fascinating that we can extend our concern to an animal we have never seen and probably never will. It tells us something fundamental about our species, offering hope for our future.

THERE ARE UNDOUBTEDLY many animals who behave altruistically, not only to their own family members or their own species but also even to others. In 1996, Binti, a female gorilla, saved a three-year-old boy who fell eighteen feet into the gorilla enclosure at the Brookfield Zoo in Illinois. He landed on the concrete and lay unconscious and badly wounded. Spectators screamed as Binti approached the boy, fearing the worst. Another female gorilla also came forward, but Binti growled at her and she left. With her own infant on her back, Binti gently picked up the boy and comforted him by patting him on the back. Cradling him in her right arm as she would her own infant, she carried him to an access entrance and handed him over to the waiting zoo personnel. One might wonder why the other gorillas might have posed a threat. Well, they were, after all, prisoners, and we know that human prisoners can often become aggressive simply because of how they are forced to live. Was Binti's action training or altruism?

Or consider that one of the most striking examples of sympathy and sensitivity to the suffering of others comes from a bonobo named Kuni at England's Twycross Zoo. When a starling hit the glass of her enclosure and lay stunned, Kuni picked up the bird with one hand, climbed into the highest tree, carefully unfolded the wings, spread them wide open, then flung the bird into the air and freedom.

These stories, which I much admire, still do not rise to the full definition of altruism, where we place our own lives in danger to help someone unrelated to us. Except for dogs, I don't know any stories of an animal risking his or her life for the sake of an animal of a different species.

ARE WE GOOD or evil at heart? What is our true nature? There is no answer, for we are all individuals, each person different from every other. Animals, too, are particular individuals, each with a distinct personality. But the huge range we find in humans is not visible in other species. Perhaps this is a result of all those qualities we saw earlier, which distinguish humans from other animals and which are not to our glory.

Even though scientists can rail all they want at how absurd the question of what our fundamental nature is, people will still go on asking it. This is because we are constantly weighing ourselves in the balance: What are we? Where do we fall? On what side? How do we measure up? What would we have done under those circumstances?

Not only do we compare ourselves to other humans, but we invariably wonder about other species as well. Do they ever find themselves in such moral quandaries? What allows elephants to wander about almost invariably peaceful in their encounters with one another and even with other animals, whereas we are constantly faced with moral choices for which we seem ill equipped?

"If only it were all so simple!" Alexander Solzhenitsyn wrote in *The Gulag Archipelago*. "If only there were evil people somewhere insidiously committing evil deeds, and it were necessary only to separate them from the rest of us and destroy them. But the line dividing good and evil cuts through the heart of every human being. And who is willing to destroy a piece of his own heart?"

This is the enlightened position, I know.[1] But I find it hard to assent to this view. The descriptions Solzhenitsyn provides in his many books of utter indifference to the suffering of others cannot be part and parcel of *every* human heart, as he seems to be saying in this passage. That said, I do find it odd that the ability to recognize and acknowledge suffering in others (including other species) appears not to be something we are all born with. What happens inside the heart of a person who watches another obviously suffering without doing anything to stop it? What obstructs the development of his empathy?

While I have spent most of my time in this book lamenting our species and what we have become (because I do not believe evil is genetic), echoing the great song by Nick Cave "People Ain't No Good," I also noted that humans and dogs seem to be the only species that care about the well-being of other species enough to put our lives at risk to protect them.

But perhaps I have let myself get carried away by claiming we are almost the only ones to understand altruism for a different species. Consider this extraordinary story: From 1972 to 1977, Captain Paul Watson served on the Greenpeace board of directors, as well as captaining and crewing many protest voyages. Soviet whalers were after sperm whales because the heat-resistant spermaceti oil found in their heads was used for lubricating intercontinental ballistic missiles. Humans were killing the largest predator that had ever lived on earth in order to create weapons with which they could kill one another. On one 1975 protest mission against the Soviet killing of sperm whales, something happened that Watson says changed his life forever: "We put ourselves between a harpoon and a whale. They fired the harpoon over our head and hit a female from the pod. She screamed; it was like a woman screaming and there were fountains of blood."

Shortly thereafter, another Soviet harpoon exploded in the head of a different whale. He was dying. He rose up, and was about to crush the dinghy Watson was in. As he came roaring up to the boat, with a trail of bloody bubbles, Watson caught the eye of the whale. "The easiest move at that point was to come right down on top of us. As I looked up at that eye, rising out of the water, an eye the size of my fist; what I saw there really changed my life forever. Because I saw understanding. He understood what we were trying to do. I saw the muscles pull, and he pulled himself back and slipped under the sea to die." So while this whale did not organize the whale equivalent of Greenpeace, he did understand the most complex thing of which we are capable: the distinction between good and bad. He knew that Watson was attempting to save the lives of his fellow whales, and he felt gratitude, even as he was dying, and made the supreme effort to avoid harming him and his altruistic crew.

There is, of late, extraordinary interest in the origins and functions of altruism. The evolutionary origins of empathy are beginning to come into focus. But modern evolutionary biologists still see altruism as reflecting a degree of genetic closeness.[2] This started, it would seem, with the biologist J. B. S. Haldane, who, as legend has it, was once asked how far he would go to save the life of another person. Haldane thought for a moment, scribbled numbers on the back of a napkin, and then answered: "I would jump into a river to save two brothers, but not one," Haldane said. "Or to save eight cousins but not seven."[3] This was moral arithmetic, and Haldane believed it was entirely scientific: we will sacrifice our life for a family member because that is how we promote our own DNA.

Perhaps this is true when confined to the back of a napkin, but in reality how many stories have we heard where a person jumps into a river to save somebody's life *only* after making the correct mathematical and genealogical calculations? Richard Alexander, one of the prime movers of evolutionary biology, makes the important point that evolution has a lot to say about why people do what they do, but he also believes that when it comes to what people *ought* to do, it says "nothing whatsoever."[4]

His views have been extremely influential and have had a great impact on one of the most celebrated of the evolutionary biologists, George C. Williams. Alexander puts the position, now accepted by most people in this discipline, as follows: "Today more than ever, natural selection can be regarded as a process that maximizes short-sighted selfishness. If one organism ever does something that benefits another it must result from either (1) an accident or malfunction, (2) kin selection, with the benefit going to a relative and partial genetic surrogate for the provider of the benefit, (3) exploitative manipulation of the giver by the receiver, or (4) reciprocity that sooner or later is profitable to the giver. The practice of charity, with net cost to the practitioner, will always be disfavored by natural selection." This is called Williams law.

It sounds harsh. It is harsh. He explains this by noting the message that "our galaxy is an infinitesimal part of the universe, the solar system a minuscule part of the galaxy, the Earth only about a hundred-thousandth part of the solar system, and the biologically relevant part of the earth only a thin film on its surface. There is nothing in this deployment of materials to suggest that there is anything of cosmic importance about what happens on Earth."[5]

But how will these laws account for the fact that people risk their lives for total strangers, even for members of a completely different species? What possible benefit, in purely biological terms, can there be for such behavior? There is no profit, there is no genetic connection, and there is no prestige to be found, no influencing others. It is pure unselfish behavior, and we see this all the time.

But now we come to the radical recognition of just what evolutionary biology and evolutionary psychology are really aiming for:

nothing less than the transformation of our species into the ultimate good species compared to all other animal species. Williams
wrote in his article, which he titled "Mother Nature Is a Wicked Old
Witch," that "most of the phenomena found in the biological world
are clearly those of selfishness and often of gross destructiveness."
He continues: "The moralizing of sentimentalists continues to work
its mischief in the use of biological material in literature intended
for the lay public [that would be you and me]. There is a steady
production of works that lead one to believe that only our own
species, and perhaps its modern representatives, regularly indulge
in conspecific killing [we kill one another], rape and other sex crimes,
or wasteful use of resources. In fact the opposite is true. Our own
species is extraordinarily benign in all these respects compared to
many others."

To prove his point Williams refers to an article he wrote in an
edition of T. H. Huxley's *Evolution and Ethics*, which gives a rather
small selection of killing, infanticide, and rape among insects,
spiders, fishes, and a few mammals.[6] Thus he writes, "In large
mammals with horns or antlers, death or debilitating injury from
fighting over females may claim five to ten percent of adult males
every breeding season." Simply taking this at face value from a
scholar of Williams's reputation would lead the lay reader to
conclude that this is true of at least a large number of mammals
with horns or antlers, but in fact the two references are for small,
quite specific populations of a given animal.

For Anna Freud, *all* human altruism was based on "altruistic
surrender," which she defined as a person giving up her own goals,
pleasure, desire, et cetera, in favor of another. It is, she claimed,
entirely based on masochism. No doubt she was thinking of her
own case, where she gave up all forms of physical gratification in
exchange for taking care of her father, Sigmund, and his child—in
this case, psychoanalysis. Anna was completely identified with

psychoanalysis her entire life, as I saw when I spent considerable time with her in London in the early 1980s.

She first wrote about altruism in her classic book *The Ego and the Mechanisms of Defence*, in which she coined the term "altruistic surrender."[7] The word *surrender* is a giveaway, for all the examples she provides come from a surrender of sexuality. The one "historic example" she gives is actually from a play by Edmond Rostand, *Cyrano de Bergerac*. Cyrano cannot marry his beautiful cousin Roxane because he believes he is too ugly, and so instead he turns his life over to his friend Christian, to whom he devotes his skill as a swordsman and his poetic abilities. At the end of the section on altruism, Anna Freud writes, "It remains an open question whether there is such a thing as a genuinely altruistic relation to one's fellow men." She says this because she limits examples to the sphere of frustrated love. I find it fascinating that, having survived the *Anschluss* in Austria, she did not provide an historical example with wider implications. Because she did not, it is not surprising that the entire notion of altruism—that is, sympathy, empathy, and compassion—remains neglected in psychoanalytic theory, as opposed to psychology in general, for which altruism has become a major topic of discussion.

The first time I met Anna Freud was in 1976, long before I became involved with her in my capacity as projects director of the *Freud Archives*. I was accompanied by my first wife, Terri Masson, a survivor of the Warsaw ghetto who had remarkable intellectual insight into World War Two and was looking forward to discussing that period with her. I was interested to hear what the two survivors would say to each other. But when Terri tried to talk about the wider topic of trauma during that dark period of human history, and the effects this trauma invariably had on the lives of survivors, Freud quickly cut her off, saying that psychoanalysis was not concerned with "the real world," but only with fantasy, and could not contribute to any kind of historical analysis.

Both Terri and I were dismayed and perplexed. How could psychoanalysis simply write off the entire external world of suffering and misery? Had I taken in the implications of what she was saying, I could have saved myself considerable grief in my later struggles with psychoanalysis as established doctrine.[8] For whatever reason, Sigmund Freud simply did not have the courage to remain with his early insights about the central nature of traumas, sexual and other, in creating later human unhappiness. This certainly had repercussions on the real lives of countless women, as I was to learn when I received many letters from women whose analysts had insisted to them that their abuse was only fantasy.

Oddly enough, the only personal comment in this rather lackluster chapter on altruism in Anna Freud's book is in a footnote referring to "meddlesome onlookers, for whom no stakes are too high." She provides the German original: "*Kiebitzer, denen kein Spiel zu hoch ist.*" A kibitzer—used primarily as a Yiddish word, not a German one—is somebody who watches a betting game and encourages higher stakes since he has no direct stake in the outcome. It is actually an interesting take on the human ability to demand sacrifice if the person who must actually bear the sacrifice is somebody else. Once again, it seems to me that Freud is mimicking her father here and refusing to recognize that true altruism exists. She posits, basically, that it *cannot* exist. This is the problem with having theories. She ought to have remembered her father's favorite saying, one he heard from Charcot when he was in Paris in 1885: "La théorie c'est bon mais ça n'empêche pas d'éxister," which means it is all well and good to have a theory, but things in the real world are something else.

Much of the modern work on altruism goes back to Haldane, one of the supreme popularizers of science and a brilliant geneticist (one of the three founders of population genetics) who helped found the modern theory of evolution. Haldane earned a double first in classics and mathematics at Oxford but made his name in biochemistry and genetics. He was called "the last man who might know all there is to be known." The science fiction writer Arthur C. Clarke described him as "the finest intellect it has ever been my privilege to know."[9] Sir Peter Medawar said Haldane "was the cleverest man I ever knew."[10]

Haldane was much interested in domestication but did not think to consider the effects on the animals themselves. So the most intelligent man who ever lived was very stupid in some areas. Consider this quote: "The evolution of the hen is an example of the law, first pointed out by a group of Soviet biologists, that a domesticated animal generally passes through several stages of exploitation. In the first stage it is of no use till it is killed. The animal is merely kept to save the trouble of hunting it. In the second stage it is used while alive, and also killed. In the third stage it is only used when alive." Sure, this is true, but deplorable. Haldane, though, thought it was fine: "The pig is still entirely in the first stage. Pigs have been selected for rapid growth and high fertility, and for little else." Haldane continues: "Beef cattle, such as the Aberdeen Angus, are also in the first stage. But as soon as cattle are bred for milk production or for pulling carts or ploughs, they pass into the second stage." What is important, though, is not what "stage" they are in, but what it means for us, and what it does to us and to our sense of compassion. That Haldane, credited with originating the modern interest in altruism, should ignore or remain ignorant of animal suffering is surprising, to say the least.

Given this, I was not surprised to see that Haldane believed killing people was "a respectable relic of primitive man," and almost certainly he made popular the idea that violence is part of human nature. In *The Inequality of Man,* he wrote about his time as a captain in the Black Watch, the legendary ferocious infantry battalion of the Royal Regiment of Scotland during the First World War:

"When I got the opportunity of killing other people during the war I enjoyed it very much, though it is now more fashionable to say that one hated every moment of it."

Less well known about Haldane is the fact that he spent the last part of his life in India writing in defense of nonviolence: "I have never done an experiment on an animal of a kind which I have not previously or subsequently done on myself; and I hope I never shall." India affected him deeply. He had pet koi fish in his garden, and when he returned to London, he could not bear the thought that somebody might kill and eat them. He became convinced that "kindness to human beings and to animals usually go together. Those who ignore suffering in animals find it easier to ignore human suffering."

India sometimes has this effect on people. After all, it is the only country in the world in which kindness and compassion to animals is mentioned in the constitution itself. Given that Buddhism, Hinduism, and Jainism have at their very heart a deep belief in *ahimsā*—that is, doing no harm—it is good to see at least one country where altruism is considered the whole point of human existence.

12 · A Billion Acts of Kindness

As you view the history of our time, turn and look at the piles of bodies, pause for a short moment. and imagine that this poor residue of flesh and bones is your father, your child, your wife, is the one you love. See yourself and those nearest to you, to whom you are devoted heart and soul, thrown naked into the dirt, tortured, starving, and killed.

—Eugen Kogon[1]

RUNNING THROUGHOUT THIS BOOK THERE HAS been a tension between two different views of the nature of man. It would almost seem that there are two kinds of people in the world: those who see the world filled with a billion acts of kindness, and those who do not. The late Harvard biologist Stephen Jay Gould put the first very well: "Rare acts of depravity seem to overwhelm our landscapes both geographical and psychological. But the ordinary human decency of a billion tiny acts of kindness, done by millions of good people, set a far more powerful counterweight, too often invisible for lack of comparable news value."[2]

For many years Gould was among the most popular and influential science writers in America. His main rival in these areas is

Richard Dawkins, a fierce critic of Gould's body of work. (Gould was no friend of evolutionary psychology or the notion of the selfish gene, calling it reductionist. He was partial to the idea of pure chance and what he called "punctuated equilibria," whereas Dawkins believes in a kind of ultra-Darwinism.)

I spent some time with Gould at Harvard in 1999. He was wonderful company. But it was clear to me that he had never participated in a war, unless you count scientific controversy as being similar to war. (Gould did.) He told me that among his most unpleasant memories were the few meetings he had had with Richard Dawkins. He said that he was nonplussed by the rage, as he called it, that Dawkins directed at him. A gentle and friendly man, Gould found it puzzling that somebody could dislike him so intensely simply because they disagreed.

This belief in general benevolence is a popular position, and it seems at first glance to make good sense. So Jeremy Rifkin, the economist and political activist and adviser to the European Parliament, begins his new book, *The Empathic Civilization*, with these cheerful words: "The dawning realization that we are a fundamentally empathic species has profound and far-reaching consequences for society." A few pages later, he says, "Life . . . is, for the most part, lived out in hundreds of small acts of kindness and generosity."[3]

Both Gould and Rifkin, like most of us, led or lead very sheltered lives. But nobody is so sheltered as not to be aware of the contrasting view, as expressed here by the French poet Charles Baudelaire in the early 1860s, before he died at the young age of 46:

It is impossible to glance through any newspaper, no matter what the day, the month or the year, without finding on every line the most frightful traces of human perversity . . . Every newspaper, from the first line to the last, is nothing but a tissue of horrors. Wars, crimes, thefts, lecheries, tortures; an orgy of universal atrocity. And it is with this loathsome appetizer that civilized man daily washes down his morning repast.

When we live under these circumstances, can we still remain optimistic? Think of Germany between 1933 and 1945. For those twelve years, those billions of tiny acts were nowhere to be found. For those years, ordinary human decency was very hard to come by. If you were a Jew living in Berlin, you were not likely to witness much kindness from anyone except your fellow sufferers. Rare were the acts of solidarity from people who were part of the dominant culture. This is true, too, of many countries under comparable dictatorships. Where were the billions of tiny acts of kindness in Rwanda during the massacres? Did the prisoners in Pol Pot's Cambodia think life was good after all?

There are exceptions of great historical import, but the people who lived through dark times emerged very much scathed by their experiences, even if they sometimes thought otherwise. I think foremost of Primo Levi, who addressed these issues in his last book, *The Drowned and the Saved*, before he killed himself in 1987. "The first news about the Nazi annihilation camps began to spread in the crucial year of 1942. They were vague pieces of information, yet in agreement with each other: they delineated a massacre of such vast proportions, of such extreme cruelty and such intricate motivation that the public was inclined to reject them because of their very enormity."

Or remember the great Austrian writer and resistance fighter Jean Améry, who was tortured in the Belgian Gestapo center at Fort Breendonk. Torture, says Améry, has an "indelible character. Whoever was tortured, stays tortured. Torture is ineradicably burned into him ... With the first blow from a policeman's fist, against which there can be no defense and which no helping hand will ward off, a part of our life ends and it can never again be revived." Améry put it starkly and unforgettably: "A slight pressure by the tool-wielding hand is enough to turn the other—along with his head, in which are perhaps stored Kant and Hegel, and all nine symphonies, and [Schopenhauer's] *The World as Will and Representation*—into a shrilly squealing piglet at slaughter." Améry, tortured in Auschwitz, Buchenwald, and Bergen-Belsen for being a Jew, realized how easily the human social contract protecting the weak could be breached with impunity. The world stood by silently, and in the end Améry committed suicide.

Are we to tell these men to take the long view? Or seek more perspective? However, the very idea of keeping perspective is not as easy to understand as one might at first think.

Certainly those in the middle of violence, or in its immediate aftermath, cannot retain their innocence with respect to a benign universe: This is from a witness at the trial of General Radislav Kristic, at The Hague's Srebrenica trial: "As a mother, I still have hope . . . How is it possible that a human being could do something like this, could destroy everything, could kill so many people? Just imagine this youngest boy I had, those little hands of his, how could they be dead? I imagine those hands picking strawberries, reading books, going to school, going on excursions. Every morning I wake up, I cover my eyes not to look at other children going to school holding hands." Her testimony was so moving that even the seasoned American prosecutor Mark Harmon could not read it aloud during his summation. He instead played the tape of her own hesitant, poignant account.

These and other eyewitness accounts are difficult to read, even more difficult to imagine, and still more difficult to understand. If we have a position about "the goodness of man," we are forced to ignore these accounts or somehow diminish their importance. That would be a grave mistake.

Of course nobody expects a person who is being tortured in Yemen or pushed out of a plane in Argentina to take the long view and say that when viewed from a great perspective, humans are capable of good. Such a person is in the hands of ruthless evil people. There is nothing banal about the evil that person is experiencing.

But, someone may object, what about Anne Frank? She embodies, if anyone does, this ability to look beyond her own circumstances. Surely her view counts just as much? Moreover, wasn't she a victim of atrocity, perhaps the single most famous victim of all time? And the single most famous quote about the Holocaust comes from this victim, and supports Gould and Solzhenitsyn, for she wrote, at the end of her diary, "In spite of everything, I still believe that people are good at heart."[4] This was written on Saturday, July 15, 1944, when Anne was fifteen years old. Two weeks later, on the morning of August 4, 1944, the German Order Police stormed the secret annex and put Anne, her older sister, Margot, her father, Otto, and her mother, Edith, on a train. The poignancy is almost unbearable. The train with the Franks on it was the last train to leave the Netherlands for Auschwitz. Just weeks before, she had written in her diary one of the saddest lines in all literature: "One day this terrible war will be over. The time will come when we will be people again, and not just Jews."

As we learn from her Dutch Jewish friend Bloeme Evers-Emden, who survived Auschwitz, Anne believed that her father had been immediately gassed (in fact, he survived the war). Her mother died of starvation, just as Anne suspected. In October, Anne and Margot were sent to Bergen Belsen. In March 1945, a typhus epidemic hit the camp. Margot, too weak to move, fell out of her bed and died on the spot. A few days later Anne Frank died, just weeks before British troops liberated the camp in April.

Would she have written these same words after she was betrayed (probably by a business associate of her father's who was a committed Nazi) and sent to a death camp, or after what she witnessed in the camps? Consider what this precocious girl had already seen. The sentence preceding the famous quote reads: "I see the world gradually being turned into a wilderness [actually the literal translation of the original should be "desert," an even starker term], I hear the ever approaching thunder, which will destroy us too, I can feel the sufferings of millions."

But even if we agree that Anne Frank did not give up her hope, at least at this point, we should also be aware that she grew up under the influence of her father, Otto Frank. Karl Josef Silberbauer was the Austrian Nazi who arrested the Franks in the attic. Simon Wiesenthal found him in 1963, eighteen years after the war. Silberbauer was once again working as a policeman in Vienna. The press pounced, but the courts were unable to proceed because Otto Frank vouched for him! "He behaved," Frank said in a declaration, "correctly" and was "simply acting on orders." Anne worshiped her father, so we can find here the seeds of her willingness to forgive.

Shortly before he died, Primo Levi wrote a memorial for the Italian prisoners of Auschwitz in which he said, "Ma non tutti gli italiani sono stati fascisti" (not all Italians were fascists). Levi meant that even though the Italian nation as a whole had joined with Germany in a fascist union, not all Italian individuals were fascists, as he illustrates in this extraordinary story from his most famous book, *If This Is a Man*:

> An Italian civilian worker brought me a piece of bread and the remainder of his ration every day for six months; he gave me a vest of his, full of patches; he wrote a postcard on my behalf to Italy and brought me the reply. For all this he neither asked nor accepted any reward, because he was good and simple and did not think that one did good for a reward . . . I believe that it was really due to Lorenzo that I am alive today; and not so much for

his material aid, as for his having constantly reminded me by his presence, by his natural and plain manner of being good, that there still existed a just world outside our own, something and someone still pure and whole, not corrupt, not savage, extraneous to hatred and terror; something difficult to define, a remote possibility of good, but for which it was worth surviving . . . But Lorenzo was a man; his humanity was pure and uncontaminated, he was outside this world of negation. Thanks to Lorenzo, I managed not to forget that I myself was a man.

Is it possible that we are, all of us, simply incapable of taking in the full impact of human misery, that we are not psychologically designed for it? If we were designed *not* to take it in, it is probably because it did not happen in most of our history. The magnitude of human misery has been increasing for the last ten thousand years but was immeasurably less before that time. That is why I believe it is wrong to speak of our species as hopelessly bound to violence— because there was a time when we were not, and that time could come again.

Epilogue: Elephant Trauma and the Promise of a Better World

Modern warfare is not natural; our bellicose human habits violate long-evolved prosocial norms shared by animals every-where, including the mighty, brainy elephant. Elephant society only fell victim to "soldier's heart" when culls, poaching, and habitat destruction shattered social structures that provided young elephants inoculation against trauma.

—Gay Bradshaw

 IN AN IMPORTANT BOOK, *Elephants on the Edge*, Gay Bradshaw demonstrates that elephants who engage in aggressive behavior toward other animals (raping and killing rhinos in Africa, for example, or killing their keepers in zoos) are responding to trauma by humans. In the case of these adolescent elephants, as young calves they were tied to their mothers' legs while their mothers were slaughtered for ivory. They grew up without family and, not surprisingly, became destructive adolescents. While elephants are not, by definition, predators (they are called "charismatic megafauna"), these big-brained, emotional animals have much to teach us with respect to living in harmony with others as well as the ill effects of disharmony.

When scientists found a polar bear who was about to give birth killed at her maternal den by another polar bear, they were puzzled. It was unprecedented. In twenty-four years of research on polar bears in the southern Beaufort Sea region of northern Alaska, and thirty-four years in northwestern Canada, they had never seen polar bears stalking, killing, or eating other polar bears. But these bears are living in a time of trauma. Because the seasons are now ice-free much longer, bears are unable to move about freely, so they cannot find enough to eat. They are starving. Human-caused climate change turns bears cannibalistic.[1]

When Susan Sontag once saw a baby elephant up close, she said she was so overwhelmed that she "sobbed and sobbed." Is this common reaction because we instinctively recognize the similarity between them and us, and then when we reflect on what we have done to these animals we are overwhelmed with guilt? We would, in my ideal world (and why not strive for one?), stop eating animals, stop experimenting on them, stop wearing them, stop exploiting them in any way, and certainly stop comparing them to us negatively. If we engaged in a fair comparison of animals and humans, we would gain a deeper understanding of where our own species has gone wrong. We can learn, too, what can be done about it, even at this late hour.

IF WE ACKNOWLEDGE that the dark side of human nature exists, and if we can abolish the ugly aspects of the us/them distinction, the benefit for the human species would be incalculable. Taking the lives of animals seriously, seeing both where we surpass them (our ability to pass on knowledge cumulatively) and where they surpass us (their general lack of ill will for others), could lead us to a better world.

I talked earlier of how Konrad Lorenz mistakenly believed that wolves never killed one another: they simply had a ritualized fight that ended when one gave up. It was an idea that appealed to people when he first published it in the early 1960s in his book *On Aggression*. But there is a kernel of truth in that idea that still remains valid. We *do* have an important lesson to learn from almost all other predators: there is a time to cede, to back down, to bend, to give in, even to walk away. Intact. Alive. This is true not just of violent encounters; even marital spats and disagreements with children can be helped if one recognizes the value of listening to the other side. We don't always have to be right, or on top, or victorious. Animals know this instinctively, it would seem, and we can learn it from them.

We have seen in an earlier chapter how a tiger took vengeance on a human who had hunted him, turning the tables and hunting the human. It is a strange story, because we do not expect concepts such as vengeance to be part of the animal world—except, perhaps, the human-animal world. If the tiger appears to be a counterexample to the thesis of my book, I nonetheless included it because I do not wish to leave the impression that I have an airtight case. I write not as a scientist, out to prove an impregnable thesis, but as somebody who has observed something of great interest.

It seems to me that the most important question we human beings can face is this: What makes us so violent to one another (never mind to other species), and is there anything to be done about it? I am attempting here to supply clues to the puzzle of why only humans, of all the millions of species on this earth, have developed an entire vocabulary around killing, with such words, concepts, and acts as *genocide, torture, murder*, and others.[2] It would be difficult to apply *any* of these terms in an animal context.

These issues are not part of an esoteric debate but are the concerns of all of us all of the time. How could it not be so, when it has to do with how we will survive in our world? As a species, we are meaning-seeking. I remember that, as a young professor of Sanskrit at the University of Toronto, I would stand in front of my three or four students and think: "Is this how I am to spend my life, reading ancient Indian texts? How will I understand my place in the universe if this is all I manage to do?" This thought propelled me to psychoanalysis, where I discovered a different but equally deep parochialism, but that is another story. Oddly enough, it was only when I began to research animal feelings that I came to my present position. I feel I have been attempting to get here all my life. I am sure that in tackling this problem, the search for the origins of human violence, I have come across the most important issue I will ever face.

I KNOW IT seems unlikely that our entire evolutionary history of the last ten thousand years will suddenly undergo a change of direction. We are not going to get rid of domestication, let alone agriculture. But if we recognize how these practices have distorted what ought to be true human nature, it will help us to move in the right direction.

One of the great examples of how our species could evolve can be seen in the forty-five years of cessation of war after the ancient Indian emperor Ashoka saw with his own eyes the devastation war caused. Ashoka ruled a territory that includes most of today's India, Pakistan, Afghanistan, and eastern parts of Iran.[3] In the year 265–64 B.C.E., he conquered the feudal republic of Kalinga (present-day Oriya) on the east coast of the Bay of Bengal. The ferocious battle has been memorialized in one of the most famous edicts ever chiseled in stone. The emperor himself had a monument erected with these ringing words, perhaps unique among the annals of warfare:

The Kalinga country was conquered by King Priyadarsi, Beloved of the Gods, in the eighth year of his reign. One hundred and fifty thousand persons were carried away captive, one hundred thousand were slain, and many times that number died. The Beloved of the Gods, conqueror of the Kalingas, is moved to remorse now. For he has felt profound sorrow and regret because the conquest of a people previously unconquered involves slaughter, death, and deportation. But Beloved of the Gods is pained even more by this—that householders of different religions who live in those countries, and who are respectful to superiors, to mother and father, to elders, and have strong loyalty towards friends, acquaintances, companions, relatives, servants and employees—that they are injured, killed or separated from their loved ones. Even those who are not affected suffer when they see friends, acquaintances, companions and relatives affected. These misfortunes befall all [as a result of war], and this pains Beloved of the Gods.

How many kings and generals have seen a battlefield strewn with thousands of dead men without shedding a tear, or feeling the slightest remorse, or feeling anything but the thrill of victory? Why did this man, feared for his cruelty, suddenly undergo such a transformation? We probably will never know, but it coincided with the emperor converting to Buddhism.

Perhaps I will be forgiven if I include one more inscription, because the topic is so dear to my heart and is also, I believe, unique in the annals of emperors: "Formerly, in the kitchen of Beloved of the Gods, King Priyadarsi, hundreds of thousands of animals were killed every day to make curry. But now with the writing of this Dhamma edict only three creatures, two peacocks and a deer are killed, and the deer not always. And in time, not even these three creatures will be killed."

LOVE IS A strong and emotive word that has been used by almost all the great poets, and then denounced by them as well for being unrealistic or at least overly sentimental. I understand why. But perhaps if we recognize one of its most important components, compassion, we can use it without shame or reservation. The world needs more compassion—for ourselves, for our species, and for other species. That way lies salvation.

Appendix I:
Human Traits Unique to Us

We alter the world of other animals such that they can no
    longer survive

Animal sacrifices

Targeted assassinations

Atrocities

Blood feuds

Causing extinctions

Enslaving other animals

Evil

Genocide

Unbridled greed

Hatred

Hunting or killing for pleasure

Injustice

Mass murder

Militaries

Paranoia

Planed exterminations

Raising other animals for food

Serial killers

Suicide
Threatening the survival of all life on earth
Tyranny
Vengeance
Wickedness

Appendix II: Human Universals

If you look at the list of universals from Donald Brown's 1991 book *Human Universals*, reproduced by Steven Pinker in *The Blank Slate* and elsewhere, we find the following characteristics of all human societies. Brown says human universals "comprise those features of culture, society, language, behavior, and psyche for which there are no known exception." I am inclined to believe that the list I have compiled from Brown's larger list is absent from almost all animal species, with a few exceptions, and, what is more important, many of these traits were probably absent from human society before the advent of agriculture and domestication. It is not a list our species can brag about. Nor do I believe it is even true, though it is widely accepted; for example, the Oedipus complex is included simply because Freud said it was universal, but that is not even universal in Western societies. It is, in fact, a figment of his imagination, conjured up to hide the reality of child sexual abuse.

Beliefs about disease
Concept of luck
Cooking
Copulation in private

Death rituals

Dream interpretation

Envy

Economic inequality

Ethnocentrism

Facial expression of contempt

Fire

Fear of death

Attempts to predict the future

Gossip

Grammar

Hairstyles

Inheritance rules

Interpreting behavior

Keeping dogs

Romantic love

Language employed to manipulate others

Magic (belief in, in order to win love)

Making comparisons

Mealtimes

Measuring

Medicine

Mood- or consciousness-altering techniques or substances

Myths

Oedipus complex

Past, present, future

Nepotism

Private inner life

Prestige (no gurus in the animal world)

Proverbs

Property

Psychological defense mechanisms

Revenge

Risk taking

Rituals

Sexual modesty

Spears

Sweets preferred

Taboos

Weapons

Attempts to control weather

Worldview

Same word for pupil of the eye in almost all languages: Hebrew, Turkish, and Spanish

Added by Pinker:

Judging others

Self-image

Sex differences in spatial cognition

Concept of precedence (how the leopard got its spots)

Appendix III: Traits Humans Have in Common with Other Animals

Sexual infidelity

Compassion

Dignity

Forbearance (with children)

Gentleness

Indulgence (with children)

Long-suffering (for our children again)

Protectiveness of young

Self-sacrifice for young

Tenderness

Toleration

Yearning for freedom

Appendix IV: Benevolent Traits Unique to Humans

Charity

Generosity

Gentle-heartedness

Graciousness

Inspirational

Large-heartedness

Moral conviction

Ability to understand the point of view of somebody else

Heroism

Philanthropy

Magnanimity

Pity

Insight

Erudition

Philosophical resignation

Sagacity

Love for mankind

Ministration to the sick

Sorrow for another's suffering (*Mitleid*)
Display of mercy (even for an enemy)
Public-spiritedness
Scholarship
Readiness to spare
Tenderheartedness
Universal goodwill
Wisdom

Appendix V: What Humans Do to Other Animals

Since this book is especially concerned with comparing violence in our species to violence in other species, it is worth reminding ourselves of the violence we inflict on those other species, unprecedented in its scope around the world today:

- We raise animals for food. For this we currently kill sixty billion land animals alone per year.
- We experiment on them for the good of our species. The Nuffield Council on Bioethics reports that, globally, experimentation is estimated to use from fifty million to one hundred million vertebrate animals annually.
- We use their fur and skin. Fifty million animals (excluding rabbits) are killed annually for fur alone, over a billion for skin (e.g., leather).
- We take their eggs. Nobody knows how many. In the United Kingdom alone it is a staggering eleven billion hens' eggs per year.
- We take their children after they are born. Hundreds of

millions of lambs, from ten weeks to four months old, are killed every year for food and to make handbags and other luxury items.

- We use their milk meant for their young for our own purposes. Around one trillion pounds of milk are taken from cows every year around the world.
- We hunt them. Hunters kill over a hundred million animals every year in the United States alone.
- We lock them into cages in zoos, rodeos, circuses, and aquaria. There are at least ten thousand zoos worldwide, with at least five million animals.

Appendix VI: The Problem with Pinker on the Problem of Human Violence

In his 2011 book *The Better Angels of Our Nature: Why Violence Has Declined*, Steven Pinker claims that the decline of violence "may be the most important thing that has ever happened in human history." That would be true *only* if violence really has declined. One way that Pinker attempts to prove his point is to assert that before historical records, when our species consisted entirely of hunter-gatherers, violence was endemic. But this is false, as has been pointed out by several historians of the origins of war, including Brian Ferguson. In fact, war probably emerged only after the advent of agriculture, between ten thousand and twelve thousand years ago. We see this clearly when we look at the ancient Middle East. Extensive remains have been found of the Natufian hunter-gatherers, who lived between about 12,800 and 10,500 years ago in what are now Israel, the West Bank, Jordan, Lebanon, and Syria. Careful analysis of 370 skeletons has turned up only two that show any signs of trauma, and nothing to suggest military action. Pinker mainly draws from present-day hunter-gatherers, whose circumstances are very different from our ancestors of a hundred thousand years ago.

But apart from the distorted version of prehistory, surely it is odd, in a book arguing that violence is decreasing all over the world, that there is little or no mention of Srebrenica, the Rwandan genocide, Pinochet in Chile, the junta in Argentina (or Brazil or Greece); no entry under colonialism, the former Yugoslavia, Haiti, Dominican Republic, or Zimbabwe's Robert Mugabe; and only one mention of Mussolini and two of apartheid, and with virtually no discussion of the violence in places such as Guatemala, the Korean War, and many other instances one can think of.[1] Pinker is able to make his claims because of the cavalier manner in which he treats most violence in the world over the past fifty years. He believes there continue to be blips of violence, but these have generally been quickly resolved. And so he writes: "Most conquests, such as the Indonesian takeover of East Timor, have been reversed as well." There is no mention of the deaths in East Timor, over 100,000 of them, according to the Truth and Reconciliation Commission (and this with a 1975 population of only 672,405 people), or the twenty-five years it took.[2] The horrendously violent partition of India (with up to one million people murdered) is not to be found in the book; Kashmir goes unmentioned, as does the war in Kosovo and the Iran-Iraq War; nor would it seem that the Soviet takeovers of Czechoslovakia and Hungary, in 1958 and 1968 respectively, are worth even a mention. The same is true of China's occupation of Tibet, which, according to Thubten Jigme Norbu, the older brother of the Dalai Lama, killed 17 percent of the entire population. So Pinker fails to mention or discuss, in a book about the alleged decline of human violence, some of the most violent episodes in our recent history.

Central to Pinker's argument is the necessity of showing that there are *today* no peaceable hunter-gatherers, because there *never* have been. He is wrong. As Richard Lee and Richard Daly write in their introduction to the *Cambridge Encyclopedia of Hunters and Gatherers*, the single most authoritative account of hunters and gatherers in modern times:

Hunter-gatherers are generally peoples who have lived until recently without the overarching discipline imposed by the state. They have lived in relatively small groups, without centralized authority, standing armies, or bureaucratic systems. Yet the evidence indicates that they have lived together surprisingly well, solving their problems among themselves largely without recourse to authority figures and without a particular propensity for violence. It was *not* the situation that Thomas Hobbes, the great seventeenth-century philosopher, described in a famous phrase as "the war of all against all." By all accounts life was not "nasty, brutish and short." . . . Most striking, the hunter-gatherers have demonstrated the remarkable ability to survive and thrive for long periods—in some cases thousands of years—without destroying their environment.

Most scholars, and especially paleoarchaeologists who have access to the data, agree and have long claimed that violence in the form of organized warfare began *only* with the advent of agriculture about ten thousand years ago. This is also de Waal's position. Even though evidence for individual murder goes back hundreds of thousands of years, absent are comparable signs of warfare (such as graveyards with weapons embedded in a large number of skeletons).

These hunter-gatherer societies mirror, to some extent, our own prehistoric past, that is, from about fifty thousand years ago until the rise of agriculture and the culture of war that followed. Pinker, in claiming this is not so, is making a serious objection.

The Semai from the Malaysian Peninsula are important to Pinker's thesis that violence among humans has declined. If a present-day hunter-gatherer society was always peaceable, this would present a serious difficulty for this thesis. So early on in his book he brings up the Semai as an example of what other scholars have called a peaceful society, something he denies. He thinks these scholars have all been hoodwinked, or at least deeply mistaken. He writes:

> The Semai are a hunting and horticulturalist tribe who were described in a book called *The Semai: A Nonviolent People of Malaya* and who go out of their way to avoid the use of force. While there aren't many Semai homicides, there aren't many Semai. When the anthropologist Bruce Knauft did the arithmetic, he found that their homicide rate was 30 per 100,000 per year, which puts it in the range of the infamously dangerous American cities in their most violent years and at three times the rate of the United States as a whole in its most violent decade.

This figure has been cited in several reviews I read of Pinker's book, as proving "case closed."

The problem is that Pinker is relying, as he admits, on an article by Bruce Knauft that used faulty data based on the seminal work by the anthropologist Robert Knox Dentan. In a 1988 article, Dentan explains how the error arose: "Knauft's impression that these data come from the 300 or so persons whom I knew personally is due to my vagueness but wrong. In fact, my account refers to a population which has increased steadily from about 16,000 in the mid-1950s, so that the murder rate would be about 0.56 per 100,000 if all cases were counted—not a high rate."

Pinker could have known this easily, not just from Dentan's own writings but also from the widely known books by Douglas P. Fry, especially *The Human Potential for Peace: An Anthropological Challenge to Assumptions about War and Violence* (Oxford University Press, 2006), where he discusses this error.

I found an actual copy of the book by Dentan and read it carefully.[3] At the very beginning of the book (p. 8) the author writes,

"The 1965 census put the Semai population at 12,748, probably a slight underestimate." Then, while discussing their nonviolent image (p. 58), he says, "Murder, of course, is almost unthinkable. Informants said there were no penalties for murder because 'it never happens, in the olden days or today.' Since a census of the Semai was first taken in 1956, not one instance of murder, attempted murder, or maiming has come to the attention of either government or hospital authorities."

Pinker should have acknowledged his error and looked elsewhere for evidence that we were a violent species long ago.[4] There is no evidence whatever that we are a less violent species today than we were several hundred or several thousand years ago. But there is good evidence that we were far less violent twenty, thirty, and fifty thousand years ago. This is the opposite of Pinker's thesis and needs to be studied in great detail, as a number of scholars interested in peace studies are doing right now.

Acknowledgments

Many people have been through this book from beginning to end, and suggested many excellent changes. I would like to thank Jenny Miller and Dana Isaacson, both of whom are freelance editors, the best I have encountered; Jackie Johnson, an editor with Bloomsbury, did a superb job; Laura Phillips supervised the copyediting and production. Sue Warga copyedited the book; she did a magnificent job and saved me from some embarrassing errors. I am also grateful to Sherry Colb, professor of law at Cornell University Law School (author of the wonderful *Mind if I Order the Cheese Burger: And Other Questions People Ask Vegans*) who was the first person to read the whole book and who made many helpful suggestions. As usual Nancy Miller, who edited the first book I ever wrote (and will probably edit the last one too!), is unique in the publishing world. Everyone who knows her adores her and I join a long list of authors grateful to her for more than words can say. My agent, Andy Ross, the much loved former owner of the legendary bookstore in Berkeley, Cody's, is a treasure; he not only sells my books, he helps in every possible way.

Notes

Preface: Can the Human Species Wake Up?

1   E. O. Wilson, *The Social Conquest of Earth* (New York: Liveright, 2012), 8.

2   This has been put more starkly by Richard Wrangham in 2004, in an influential statement claiming, "Selection has favored a human tendency to identify enemies, and draw moral divides, and exploit weaknesses pitilessly across boundaries. Among hunter-gatherer societies, inner city gangs, and volunteer militias at the fringes of contested national territories, there are similar patterns of violence. The spontaneous aggressiveness of humans is a harsh product of natural selection; part of an evolutionary morality that revels in short-term victory for one's own community without regard for the greater good." ("Killer Species," *Daedalus* (Fall 2004): 25–35.)

3   Howard Garrett, a distinguished expert on orcas who runs the Orca Network website, writes me: "Even when orcas were being captured, when divers and handlers were in the water or in small boats among the orcas during capture operations, as the mothers were being poked and driven away with sharpened poles while their young offspring were being wrapped in nets and forced into slings, never did the mothers or calves or any of the accompanying whales, male or female, strike out with even the slightest shove or swing of a fluke. This exemplary restraint is the norm among all the many diverse communities of orcas worldwide, whether they specialize in foraging for fish or hunting and killing 8,000-pound sea lions. I can't explain this reticence even to defend themselves when threatened or attacked by humans, but the record stands: orcas in natural habitats do not harm humans." The interesting question arises as to whether orcas would behave this way to *other*, nonhuman predators. We

may never know, since no other animal *except* humans is foolish enough to attack a full-grown orca. Orcas do not attack animals they do not eat.

4 It has proven surprisingly difficult to find out exactly how many orcas humans have killed over the last hundred years. Several experts I asked believed it was very few, as orcas have been targeted primarily by the aquaria industry rather than whalers. But Ingrid Visser, one of the world's leading authorities begs to differ. She has done some preliminary research for me in her database and has come up with these articles showing that orcas have been killed in the thousands, perhaps the tens of thousands: M. Nishiwaki and C. Handa, "Killer Whales Caught in the Coastal Waters off Japan for Recent 10 Years," *Scientific Reports of the Whales Research Institute* 13 (1958): 85–96; R. R. Reeves and E. Mitchell, "Killer Whale Sightings and Takes by American Pelagic Whalers in the North Atlantic," *Rit Fiskideildar* 11 (1988): 7–23; J. Sigurjonsson and S. Leatherwood, "The Icelandic Live-Capture Fishery for Killer Whales, 1976–1988," *Rit Fiskideildar* 11 (1988): 307–16; D. Vongraven and A. Bisther, "Possible Effects of Previous Catch on the Present Population of Norwegian Killer Whales (*Orcinus orca*)," in A. S. Blix, L. Walløe, and Ø. Ulltang, eds., *Whales, Seals, Fish and Man*, 177–79 (Amsterdam: Elsevier, 1996).

5 Eric Schlosser ("The Most Dangerous Job in America," *Mother Jones*, August 2001) and others have shown just how physically dangerous work in a slaughterhouse is: "The rate of cumulative trauma injuries in meatpacking is the highest of any American industry. It is about 33 times higher than the national average." *Fast Food Nation*, both the book and the film, elaborates on this. There is, more recently, much research on the psychological cost of this kind of work. See Jennifer Dillard, "A Slaughterhouse Nightmare: Psychological Harm Suffered by Slaughterhouse Employees and the Possibility of Redress Through Legal Reform," *Georgetown Journal on Poverty Law and Policy*, forthcoming, but available at http://papers.ssrn.com/sol3/papers.cfm?abstract_id=1016401.

1. Crocodiles and Us

1 For more about her views, see the piece on her by Martin Mulligan and Stuart Hill in *Ecological Pioneers* (Cambridge: Cambridge University Press, 2001), 274–300.

2 Her article about this experience is widely available on the Internet, in several versions, and is also published in J. O'Reilly, S. O'Reilly, and R. Sterling, eds., *The Ultimate Journey: Inspiring Stories of Living and Dying* (San Francisco:

Travelers' Tales, 2000), 128–46. A longer account is found in *Terra Nova* 1, 3 (1996): 32–44. See too Val Plumwood, "Wilderness Skepticism and Wilderness Dualism," in J. Baird Callicott and Michael P. Nelson, eds., *The Great New Wilderness Debate* (Athens: University of Georgia Press, 1998), 652–90.

3 Plumwood died in 2008, at the age of sixty-seven, on her wilderness property outside of Canberra, under somewhat mysterious circumstances. At first friends thought a spider bit her. (It wouldn't have been her first poisonous spider bite.) She had called a friend to say she was feeling a bit odd. Others thought it was an eastern brown snake that killed Plumwood with its deadly bite. But it seems it was a stroke after all that finally came for her, just as she was writing a book about death.

4 I am reminded of the words of Arthur Schopenhauer: "Since there is more pain than pleasure on earth, every satisfaction is only transitory, creating new desires and new distresses, and the agony of the devoured animal is always far greater than the pleasure of the devourer."

5 Tom Regan, *The Case for Animal Rights* (Berkeley: University of California Press, 2004). He argues that every creature, animal or human, has inherent value, and has the experience of "being the subject of a life," that is, has a biography just as we do, and in which what happens matters very much to them, just as it does to us whether it matters or not to anyone else. This has proved a very rich idea for many people, and he has expanded upon it in *Empty Cages: Facing the Challenge of Animal Rights* (Lanham, MD: Rowman and Littlefield, 2004), for which I wrote a preface.

2. "The Other"

1 Sigmund Freud, "Group Psychology and the Analysis of the Ego" in *The Standard Edition of the Complete Psychological Works of Sigmund Freud*, ed. James Strachey and Anna Freud (London: Hogarth Press, 1955), 18:101.

2 L. David Mech, "Alpha Status, Dominance, and Division of Labor in Wolf Packs," *Canadian Journal of Zoology* 77 (1999): 1196–203. You may wonder if rigid hierarchy applies to dogs, perhaps misled by some of Cesar Millan's shows. For a corrective, I urge you to see the fine article by Mark Derr, "Pack of Lies," *New York Times*, August 31, 2006.

3 See Laurence R. Gesquiere et al., "Life at the Top: Rank and Stress in Wild Male Baboons," *Science* 3333, no. 6040 (July 15, 2011): 357–60.

4 Joan Dunayer has written about this in *Animal Equality: Language and Liberation* (Derwood, MD: Ryce, 2001).

5 See Zoë Oldenbourg, *Massacre at Montségur: A History of the Albigensian Crusade* (London: Weidenfeld and Nicolson, 1961). She describes the massacre of four hundred people as the "largest single holocaust during the entire Crusade" (149). The fact that the four hundred "heretics" who were burned by a large crowd *cum ingenti gaudio* ("with great joy") went to their death with dignity was simply proof to the authorities that they were obdurate in their crime.

3. Conformity

1 An inspiring book on this topic is Eyal Press, *Beautiful Souls: Saying No, Breaking Ranks, and Heeding the Voice of Conscience in Dark Times* (New York: Farrar, Straus and Giroux, 2012).

2 The story is "Of That Which Happened to a King and Three Impostors." It comes from *Count Lucanor; of the Fifty Pleasant Stories of Patronio, written by the Prince Don Juan Manuel and first done into English by James York, M.D.* (London: Gibbings, 1899), 42–63. It is available in a modern retelling in the collection by Idries Shah, *World Tales* (New York: Harcourt Brace Jovanovich, 1979).

3 See the excellent book by Susan McCarthy, *Becoming a Tiger: How Baby Animals Learn to Live in the Wild* (New York: Harper, 2004).

4 Cynthia Moss, widely regarded as the world's leading authority on elephants, writes to me, "In a natural, free-ranging population one elephant killing another is very, very rare."

5 See Charles Siebert, "Watching Whales Watching Us," *New York Times*, July 8, 2009.

6 I. Visser and D. Fertl, "Stranding, Resighting and Boat Strike of a Killer Whale (*Orcinus orca*) off New Zealand," *Aquatic Mammals* 26, 3 (2000): 232–40.

7 See Robert Foley, "The Adaptive Legacy of Human Evolution: A Search for the Environment of Evolutionary Adaptedness," *Evolutionary Anthropology* 4, 6 (1995–96): 194–203.

8 "Throughout history the majority of men on the battle-field would *not* attempt to kill the enemy, even to save their own lives or the lives of their friends." This is from the influential book by Lt. Col. Dave Grossman, *On Killing: The Psychological Cost of Learning to Kill in War and Society* (Boston: Little, Brown, 1996), 4.

9 Jared Diamond, *The Third Chimpanzee: The Evolution and Future of the Human Animal* (New York: HarperCollins, 1992), 386.

10 Jane Goodall, *The Chimpanzees of Gombe: Patterns of Behavior* (Cambridge, MA: Belknap Press, 1986), 534.

11 I talk about bonobos (aka pygmy chimpanzees) later. Suffice it to say that Ian Parker's infamous article "Swingers," *New Yorker*, July 30, 2007, 48–61, in which it was claimed that bonobos are as aggressive and murderous as chimpanzees, has been refuted by none other than the leading authority on bonobos, Frans de Waal, in "Bonobos, Left and Right: Primate Politics Heats Up Again as Liberals and Conservatives Spindoctor Science," *eSkeptic*, 2008, www.skeptic.com/eskeptic/07-08-08, where he writes: "The most important fact, which has remained unchanged over the last three decades of bonobo research, is that there exist no confirmed reports of lethal aggression, neither from the field nor from captivity."

4. Cruelty

1 Whenever I say this to audiences, somebody is bound to bring up cats, who appear to be tormenting mice before they eat them. The subject has been addressed by many other authors, and the general consensus, which I share, is that this is *not* torture. It is that cats, being domesticated, are not entirely sure what to do with prey. Sometimes when I see my cats engage in what looks like torture (which I always stop), they have a slightly puzzled look on their face, as if they don't entirely know why they are doing what they are doing. Instinct is present, but the "cultural" context, which in the wild they would get from their mother, is absent. But even in nature, parents often teach their young to hunt by catch and release, which we may be seeing in cats. Dogs, too, will often catch a bird, then drop her and look confused: "Now what?"

2 Susan Hatters Friedman, Sarah McCue Horwitz, and Phillip J. Resnick, "Child Murder by Mothers: A Critical Analysis of the Current State of Knowledge and a Research Agenda," *American Journal of Psychiatry* 162 (September 2005): 1578–87.

3 Warren B. Ballard, Ludwig N. Carbyn, and Douglas W. Smith, "Wolf Interactions with Non-prey," in *Wolves: Behavior, Ecology, and Conservation*, ed. L. David Mech and Luigi Boitani (Chicago: University of Chicago Press, 2003), 259–71.

4 Robert L. Pitman, "Killer Whale Predation on Sperm Whales: Observations and Implications," *Marine Mammal Science* 17, 3 (2001): 494–507.

5 Available on YouTube: http://www.youtube.com/watch?v=ELm8yRxAK9o.

6 "It's an amazing, complex, highly evolved substance. It's the only food on the planet that's really meant to be eaten by humans." Florence Williams, *Breasts: A Natural and Unnatural History* (New York: W. W. Norton & Company, 2012).

7 John K. B. Ford, Graeme M. Ellis, and Kenneth C. Balcomb, "Killer Whales, Ships, and Care-Giving Behaviour," *Killer Whales* (Vancouver: University of British Columbia Press, 1994).

8 L. Rendell and H. Whitehead, "Culture in Whales and Dolphins," *Behavioral and Brain Sciences* 24, 2 (2001): 309–82.

9 She writes me, "Unlike most other mammals, who have four cortical lobes, cetacean brains are composed of three concentric tiers of tissue that are still called lobes. It is another layout, if you will. Among these tiers is the paralimbic lobe—which lies between the limbic and supralimbic regions. This is a unique arrangement among mammals and no one knows why it is the way it is or what the paralimbic region actually does." It may well be that we have discovered a completely different order of intelligence in the ocean. I am tempted to call it "superior," precisely because it has not been used for purposes of making war.

10 Jared Diamond, "The Worst Mistake in the History of the Human Race," *Discover*, May 1987, 64–66. Diamond takes his cue from the work of George Armelagos, professor of anthropology at Emory University, in G. Armelagos and M. N. Cohen, *Paleopathology at the Origin of Agriculture* (Orlando, FL: Academic Press, 1984). See too his article "Disease in Human Evolutio: The Re-emergence of Infectious Disease in the Third Epidemiological Transition," where he concludes, "We live in a time where there exists a virtual viral super-highway, bringing people into contact with pathogens that affect our adaptation. The present pattern reflects an evolutionary trend that can be traced to the beginning of primary food production." *National Museum of Natural History Bulletin for Teachers* 18, 3 (Fall 1996), and his "Human Evolution and the Evolution of Human Disease," *Ethnicity and Disease* 1, 1 (1991): 21–26.

11 My friend Sherry Colb reminds me that Plato predicted something like this in *The Republic*, where Socrates responds to Glaucon's insistence that the ruling class must eat animals. Then, said Socrates, there would have to be armies to guard the large amount of land needed for livestock, and lawyers for disputes surrounding land boundaries, and doctors to handle the sickness that comes of eating that way.

12 See my *The Pig Who Sang to the Moon: The Emotional World of Farm Animals* (New York: Ballantine Books, 2003). The classic book on domestication, and still the best, in my opinion, remains F. E. Zeuner, *A History of Domesticated Animals* (London: Hutchinson, 1963). See too J. Clutton-Brock, ed., *The Walking Larder: Patterns of Domestication, Pastoralism, and Predation* (London: Unwin Hyman, 1989), and J. Clutton-Brock, *A Natural History of Domesticated Mammals* (Cambridge: Cambridge University Press, 1999).

13 See R. Lockwood and F. R. Ascione, eds., *Cruelty to Animals and Interpersonal Violence: Readings in Research and Application* (West Lafayette, IN: Purdue University Press, 1998), and also A. Arluke and R. Lockwood, eds., special issue of *Society and Animals*, 5, 3 (1997).

5. War

1 Alexander Solzhenitsyn, *The Gulag Archipelago* (New York: Harper Perennial, 2007), 2:49.

2 See Pat Shipman, "Why Do Rape and Pedophilia Exist?" November 29, 2011, *Animal Connection* (blog), *Psychology Today*, www.psychologytoday.com/blog/the-animal-connection/201111/why-do-rape-and-pedophilia-exist.

3 Knowing dogs as I do, of course I would say that each dog is an individual. Am I really right, though, in claiming this is unique to dogs, or at least that it is more pronounced in dogs? Would not somebody who was deeply familiar with lions or any other large predator say the same? I stand willing to be corrected here.

4 Dale Peterson and Jane Goodall, *Visions of Caliban: On Chimpanzees and People* (Boston: Houghton Mifflin, 1993), 282.

5 See his influential but controversial book, written with Dale Peterson: *Demonic Males: Apes and the Origins of Human Violence* (Boston: Houghton Mifflin, 1996).

6 Jane Goodall, *The Chimpanzee: The Living Link Between "Man" and "Beast"* (Edinburgh: Edinburgh University Press, 1992), 15.

7 Jane Goodall, *Through a Window: My Thirty Years with the Chimpanzees of Gombe* (Boston: Houghton Mifflin, 1990), 108–09.

8 Jane Goodall, *In the Shadow of Man* (Boston: Houghton Mifflin, 1971), 143. Sherry Colb, after reading this, wrote to me: "The parallel to human agriculture seems very striking here. Once the animals (or humans) have a steady source of food, they experience a sort of 'endowment effect' with respect to the food they receive that leads them to feel threatened if anyone else wants the food (even if they are no longer hungry for it and have no use for it)."

9 Jane Goodall, *The Chimpanzees of Gombe: Patterns of Behavior* (Cambridge, MA: Harvard University Press, 1986).

10 These are the main articles presenting the evidence for this view: C. Boesch, J. Head, N. Tagg, M. Arandjelovic, L. Vigilant, and M. M. Robbins, "Fatal Chimpanzee Attack in Loango National Park, Gabon," *International Journal of Primatology* 28 (2007): 1025–34; C. Boesch, C. Crockford, I. Herbinger, R.

Wittig, Y. Moebius, and E. Normand, "Intergroup Conflicts Among Chimpanzees in Tai National Park: Lethal Violence and the Female Perspective," *American Journal of Primatology* 70 (2008): 519–32; D. P. Watts, M. N. Muller, S. A. Amsler, G. Mbabazi, and J. C. Mitani, "Lethal Inter-Group Aggression by Chimpanzees in Kibale National Park, Uganda," *American Journal of Primatology* 68 (2006): 161–80; R. W. Wrangham, M. L. Wilson, and M. N. Muller, "Comparative Rates of Aggression in Chimpanzees and Humans," *Primates* 47 (2006): 14–26; M. L. Wilson, W. R. Wallauer, and A. E. Pusey, "New Cases of Intergroup Violence Among Chimpanzees in Gombe National Park, Tanzania," *International Journal of Primatology* 25 (2004): 523–49.

11 R. B. Zajonc, "The Zoomorphism of Human Collective Violence," in Leonard S. Newman and Ralph Erber, eds., *Understanding Genocide: The Social Psychology of the Holocaust* (New York: Oxford University Press, 2002), 222–38. This is a very hard-hitting article.

12 Barbara Fruth and Gottfried Hohmann, "How Bonobos Handle Hunts and Harvests: Why Share Food?" in *Behaviour Diversity in Chimpanzees and Bonobos*, ed. Christophe Boesch, Gottfried Hohmann and Linda F. Marchant (Cambridge: Cambridge University Press, 2002), 233.

6. Killing

1 See G. McBride et al., "The Social Organization and Behaviour of the Feral Domestic Fowl," *Animal Behaviour Monographs*, Part 3 (London: Baillière, Tindall and Cassell, 1969). This is a study of the behavior and social organization of a population of feral domestic fowls (chickens), found on an uninhabited island off the coast of Queensland in Australia. The study makes a point of noting that the researchers saw no direct physical encounters between roosters during the several months of observing them. The person who knows the most about domestic chickens is Dr. Karen Davis, who runs a well-regarded sanctuary for chickens and has published widely. Here is her comment from her site: "My personal experience with our sanctuary roosters confirms the literature I've read about wild and feral chickens documenting that the majority of roosters do not physically and compulsively attack one another. Chickens maintain a social order in which every member of the flock has a place and finds a place. During the day our roosters and hens break up into small, fluctuating groups that are somewhat, but by no means, rigidly territorial." Karen Davis, "The Social Life of Chickens," 2009, United Poultry Concerns website, www.upc-online.org/thinking/social_life_of_chickens.html.

2 Many farmers claim they have to debeak chickens because otherwise they would peck one another to death, suggesting they are naturally violent. But just as in the case of cock fighting, the violence is entirely artificial, caused by overcrowding in this case, where chickens would never confront such conditions in the wild; normally they simply walk away rather than fight. *We* are the source of the violence, not chickens.

3 An informative article on cockfighting in the United States is Deborah Kennedy, "Why Cockfighting Persists," *Salon*, January 22, 2010, http://www.salon.com/2012/01/22/cockfighting_barbarism_or_tradition.

4 I take this information from the authoritative *The New Encyclopedia of Mammals* (London: Oxford University Press, 2001), 534. See too Jonathan Balcombe's book *Second Nature: The Inner Lives of Animals* (New York: Palgrave Macmillan, 2011).

5 Gabriela Villanueva, "The Story of Ferdinand: The Implication of a Peaceful Bull," 2009. ECLS Student Scholarship Paper 6, http://scholar.oxy.edu/ecls_student/6.

6 Ethologists confirm that the crying out of the bull is a social reaction: the bull is calling for its herd mates to come and help, just as humans scream in panic at a terrible event, such as an earthquake or an attack.

7 See the fine article by Jordi Casamitjana, "The Suffering of 'Bullfighting' Bulls," CAS International, www.cas-international.org/en/home/suffering-of-bulls-and-horses/the-suffering-of-bulls.

8 John Vaillant, *The Tiger: A True Story of Vengeance and Survival* (New York: Vintage, 2011).

9 Theodore N. Bailey, *The African Leopard: Ecology and Behavior of a Solitary Felid* (New York: Columbia University Press, 1993).

10 R. F. Ewer, *The Carnivores* (Ithaca, NY: Cornell University Press, 1973), 292.

11 Quoted by Deirdre Jackson, *Lion* (London: Reaktion Books, 2010), 28.

12 Donna Hart, "Humans as Prey," *Chronicle of Higher Education* 52, 33 (2006).

7. Hatred

1 When I was studying Pali, the language of early Buddhism, I read this in one of the early Pali texts, the *Dhammapada*, and it never occurred to me to question it. In fact, these are probably not the words of the Buddha himself, but what was later ascribed to him.

2 Richard Dawkins, for example, agrees: "I conclude that we have no general reason to think that non-human animals feel pain less acutely than we do, and we should

in any case give them the benefit of the doubt. Practices such as branding cattle, castration without anaesthetic, and bullfighting should be treated as morally equivalent to doing the same thing to human beings." Earlier in the essay, he maintains that some animals may well feel pain more powerfully than humans do, for good evolutionary reasons, since they are not equipped to reason about the pain. Richard Dawkins, "But Can They Suffer?" BoingBoing.com, June 30, 2011, http://boingboing.net/2011/06/30/richard-dawkins-on-v.html.

3 I highly recommend the book Juliet Eilperin, *Demon Fish: Travels Through the Hidden World of Sharks* (London: Duckworth, 2012). A lively review by Theo Tait, called "Don't Wear Yum-Yum Yellow," *London Review of Books* 34, 15 (August 2, 2012), has this great passage: "Yet people are stubbornly irrational. As one exasperated scientific paper concluded: 'Even though shark attacks are a minor cause of mortality for humans, this phenomenon receives an inordinate amount of media cover and interest, probably due to humans' psychological abhorrence of being eaten alive.' Yes, I imagine that weird hang-up has something to do with it."

4 Stephen Herrero, Andrew Higgins, James E. Cardoza, Laura I. Hajduk, and Tom S. Smith, "Fatal Attacks by American Black Bear on People: 1900–2009," *Journal of Wildlife Management*, April 2011.

5 In 2004, according to the Geneva Declaration on Armed Violence, humans killed approximately 490,000 other humans worldwide.

6 Bertrand Russell wrote in *The Conquest of Happiness* (Sydney: Allen & Unwin, 1930): "Whenever you happen to take your children to the Zoo you may observe in the eyes of the apes, when they are not performing gymnastic feats or cracking nuts, a strange strained sadness. One can almost imagine that they feel they ought to become men, but cannot discover the secret of how to do it." But the great philosopher overlooked the obvious. They were sad because they were imprisoned, not because they wanted to be human.

7 Nick Jans, *The Grizzly Maze: Timothy Treadwell's Fatal Obsession with Alaskan Bears* (New York: Penguin, 2006). The author of this fine book said that what Treadwell was doing was "incredibly wrong-headed, but right-hearted."

8 On the other hand, many people were astounded to see a video of a polar bear playing with dogs: http://morris108.wordpress.com/2008/08/31/video-wild-polar-bears-playing-with-husky-dogs. Play, it would seem, spans the species barrier. I can never get enough of thinking about what it means that my dog, like any dog, adores playing with me. I guess the polar bears felt the same way.

9 See Mietje Germonpre and Riku Hamalainen, "Fossil Bear Bones in the Belgian Upper Paleolithic: The Possibility of a Bear-Ceremonialism," *Arctic Anthropology* 44, 2 (2007): 1–30. I am grateful to Pat Shipman for this reference.

10 Bears rarely "hunt" humans. We are, obviously, not their usual prey. Given a choice, most bears will avoid humans. Timothy Floyd from the Department of Orthopedic Surgery at Johns Hopkins University School of Medicine, in a thorough review, wrote: "Contrary to popular folklore perpetuated by film documentaries, polar bears are largely indifferent to humans and often demonstrate behavior that is more curious than aggressive. In his 85-year review of bear attacks in Alaska, Middaugh found only one incident of human injury and no fatalities from polar bears." Timothy Floyd, "Bear-Inflicted Human Injury and Fatality," *Wilderness and Environmental Medicine* 10 (1999): 75–87.

11 Floyd, "Bear-Inflicted Human Injury and Fatality," documents the number of incidents involving polar bears up until that time. Over a fifteen-year period in Svalbard, Norway, researchers documented polar bears killing one person and injuring three others. In a twenty-year period in Canada, six human deaths and fourteen injuries were attributed to polar bears.

8. Exploitation

1 In an interview with the *Independent* of London about *Sacred Hunger* in 1992—two years after Prime Minister Thatcher left office—he elaborated. "As I wrote I began to see more strongly that there were inescapable analogies," Unsworth said. "You couldn't really live through the '80s without feeling how crass and distasteful some of the economic doctrines were. The slave trade is a perfect model for that kind of total devotion to the profit motive without reckoning the human consequences." Cited in Martin Childs, "Barry Unsworth: Historical Novelist Who Won the Booker Prize," *Independent*, June 9, 2012.

2 Joseph Stiglitz, *The Price of Inequality: The Avoidable Causes and Hidden Costs of Inequality* (New York: W. W. Norton, 2012). There is a chapter about pleonectic, or overreaching, greed, "the heart of Greek vices," in Melissa Lane, *Eco-Republic: Ancient Thinking for a Green Age* (Oxford: Peter Lane, 2011).

3 He wrote: "I could not have believed how wide was the difference between savage and civilized man: it is greater than between a wild and domesticated animal." It is definitely worth reading his entire comments. One Internet source is www.literature.org/authors/darwin-charles/the-voyage-of-the-beagle/chapter-10.html. When Darwin saw some other Fuegians on the other side of the island who were evidently poorer, he was disdainful to an extraordinary degree: "Viewing such men, one can hardly make one's self believe that they

are fellow-creatures, and inhabitants of the same world. It is a common subject of conjecture what pleasure in life some of the lower animals can enjoy: how much more reasonably the same question may be asked with respect to these barbarians."

4 According to Allan Keiler, a professor of musicology at Brandeis University (but who has a Ph.D. in linguistics from Harvard and is very knowledgeable about linguistics): "From the Chomskyan perspective, all languages are equal in the sense that they are derived or controlled by a fixed set of underlying structures from which languages can't deviate. But languages can differ in terms of complexity and sophistication, if one is clear about what one means. Some languages, like Georgian, for example, have a very complex morphological system, that is, much longer paradigms of forms. You could argue that in this regard Georgian is more complicated than other, less inflected languages. But then other languages manage to do the same things as Georgian does with its paradigms in different ways. What you want to say is the language Darwin was talking about was in the fullest sense a natural language."

5 See Sven Lindqvist's book *Terra Nullius: A Journey Through No One's Land* (New York: New Press, 2007). He points out that it was only in 1967 that Aboriginals were even included in the national census.

6 See A. Dirk Moses, ed., *Genocide and Settler Society: Frontier Violence and Stolen Indigenous Children in Australian History* (New York: Berghahn Books, 2004).

7 Jim Mason, "Animals: From Souls and the Sacred in Prehistoric Times to Symbols and Slaves in Antiquity," in *A Cultural History of Animals in Antiquity*, ed. Linda Kalof (Oxford: Berg, 2007), 32.

8 See Pat Shipman "Do the Eyes Have It?" *American Scientist* 100, 3 (May-June 2012), 198. For the articles on dogs from thirty-five thousand years ago, see M. Germonpré et al., "Palaeolithic Dog Skulls at the Gravettian Predmostí Site, the Czech Republic," *Journal of Archaeological Science* 39 (2012): 184–202. Also M. Germonpré et al., "Fossil Dogs and Wolves from Palaeolithic Sites in Belgium, the Ukraine and Russia: Osteometry, Ancient DNA and Stable Isotopes," *Journal of Archaeological Science* 36 (2009): 473–90.

9 See Robert K. Wayne et al., "Multiple and Ancient Origins of the Domestic Dog," *Science* 276 (June 13, 1997).

10 Richard Klein, *The Dawn of Human Culture* (New York: John Wiley and Sons, 2009).

11 "By 4,500 years ago, all the main species of domestic animals present in the world today had been incorporated into human societies." Juliet Clutton-Brock, "How Domestic Animals Have Shaped the Development of Human

Societies," in *A Cultural History of Animals in Antiquity*, ed. Linda Kalof (Oxford: Berg, 2007). I follow her dating in the dates I give above.

12 Arslan Humbaraci and Nicole Muchnik, *Portugal's African Wars* (New York: Joseph Okpaku, 1974).

13 See L. David Mech and Rolf O. Peterson, "Wolf-Prey Relations," in *Wolves: Behavior, Ecology, and Conservation*, ed. L. David Mech and Luigi Boitani (Chicago: University of Chicago Press, 2003). Cf. p. 145: "Programmed to kill whenever possible because it is rarely possible to kill, wolves automatically take advantage of an unusual opportunity."

9. Indifference

1 The polar opposite of this is the group of young people at the University of Munich called the White Rose (there is a wonderful film about this, and several good books), who distributed leaflets against the Nazis, the very same leaflets that the Allies dropped from planes all over Germany after the brave young men and women, including the brother and sister Hans and Sophie Scholl, were arrested and beheaded by the Gestapo. Claude Lanzmann at the beginning of his memoir, *The Patagonian Hare* (Farrar, Straus and Giroux, 2013), says that every time he thinks about this, he cries. They are honored heroes today in Germany.

2 From *The Letters of Thomas Mann, 1889–1955*, ed. and trans. Richard and Clara Winston (Berkeley: University of California Press, 1970). It was no surprise to me that Campbell was both extremely conservative and elitist, and a Jungian. Jung declared in a 1937 interview: "The S.S. men are being transformed into a caste of knights ruling sixty million natives . . . There is no more ideal form of government than a decent form of oligarchy—call it aristocracy if you prefer."

3 See Leo Goldberger, ed., *The Rescue of the Danish Jews: Moral Courage under Stress* (New York University Press, 1987).

4 For a full, fascinating, and sympathetic account, see Susan Zuccotti, *The Italians and the Holocaust: Persecution, Rescue, and Survival* (New York: Basic Books, 1987).

5 Matt Ridley claims this is their only function. See *The Origins of Virtue: Human Instincts and the Evolution of Cooperation* (New York: Penguin, 1997), 176.

6 Slavoj Žižek, *Violence: Six Sideways Reflections* (London, Profile Books, 2008), 46.

7 See Brian Victoria, *Zen at War* (Lanham, MD: Rowman and Littlefield, 2006).

8 Martin Gansberg, "Thirty Eight Who Saw Murder Didn't Call the Police," *New York Times*, March 27, 1964.

9 A. R. Rosenthal, *Thirty Eight Witnesses: The Kitty Genovese Case* (Berkeley: University of California Press, 1999 [1964]).

10 Sherry Colb, professor of law at UCLA after reading this chapter, wrote to remind me that a good example of the bystander effect is evident in police failure to do anything about domestic violence, despite its illegality, for many years. The law had to make it a "mandatory arrest" offense before police began taking domestic violence seriously. In other words, they would arrive at a scene in which they knew a woman would be further battered once they left, and they nonetheless left without truly intervening.

11 Cited in Jim Rasenberger, "Kitty, 40 Years Later," *New York Times*, February 8, 2004.

12 F. Cherry has pointed out the culture of violence against women missed by the commentators in *The Stubborn Particulars of Social Psychology* (London: Routledge, 1995).

13 R. Manning, M. Levine, and A. Collins, "The Kitty Genovese Murder and the Social Psychology of Helping: The Parable of the 38 Witnesses," *American Psychologist* 62, 6 (2007): 555–62.

14 Rasenberger, "Kitty, 40 Years Later."

15 The account is from A. G. Sulzberger and Mick Meenan, "Questions Surround a Delay in Help for a Dying Man," *New York Times*, April 25, 2010. It still seems to be the case that only one out of four people will even respond to a public episode of child abuse. The first article on this topic is by C. A. Christy and H. Voigt, "Bystander Responses to Public Episodes of Child Abuse," *Journal of Applied Social Psychology* 24, 9 (1994): 824–47. They retell the terrifying story of little James Bulger. In a bustling Liverpool shopping center, two-year-old James Bulger, restless and tearful, wanders from his mother's side. He drifts off into the crowd and is welcomed by two ten-year-old boys who drag James out of the shopping center. On a journey of several miles through city streets, witnesses see the tearful toddler being shoved, kicked, and thrown into the air by his cruel companions. About sixty people view this conspicuous threesome. No one intervenes. The little boy is later beaten to death with bricks and clubs by the two boys, who deposit his lifeless body on a railroad track, where a final hideous fate ensues. ("Witnesses Track 2-Year-Old from Mall to his Death," *San Francisco Chronicle*, November 5, 1993, p. 16.)

16 Zimbardo's research is different, and his point that even pacifist undergraduates would, within a short time, become abusive prison guards simply because of the role they were assigned is interesting. See his recent book, *The Lucifer*

Effect (Random House, 2008). Still, I believe Zimbardo would have learned more by visiting real prisons rather than inventing a situation that no doubt some of the players considered just that, an invention.

17 R. A. Spitz, "Hospitalism—An Inquiry into the Genesis of Psychiatric Conditions in Early Childhood," *Psychoanalytic Study of the Child* 1 (1945): 53–74.

18 Moreover, not everyone who repeated Milgram's experiment got the same results. In Australia, far fewer people agreed to shock, and when women were asked to shock, only 14 percent did so. People differ.

19 Seligman was heavily involved in CIA torture protocols—the psychologists who devised the torture explicitly mentioned Seligman and his research on dogs, and Seligman even gave a notorious lecture to the navy training school involved.

20 Robert van Reekum, Donald T. Stuss, and Laurie Ostrander, "Apathy: Why Care?" *Journal of Neuropsychiatry and Clinical Neurosciences* 17 (2005): 7–19.

21 Donna Hart and Robert W. Sussman, *Man the Hunted: Primates, Predators, and Human Evolution* (Boulder, CO: Westview Press, 2005).

22 I deliberately use the word *wild* because domesticated animals, when subjected to human cruelty, can become psychopathic. Think of fighting dogs. They are not representative of animals in the wild.

23 Paul Babiak and Robert D. Hare, *Snakes in Suits: When Psychopaths Go to Work* (New York: HarperCollins, 2006), 91.

24 Dale Peterson, *The Moral Lives of Animals* (New York: Bloomsbury, 2011), 220. This example is taken from Joyce Poole, *Coming of Age with Elephants: A Memoir* (New York: Hyperion, 1996). Frans de Waal also tells it in *The Age of Empathy: Nature's Lessons for a Kinder Society* (New York: Crown, 2009), 142.

25 See her delightful book *Beast and Man: The Roots of Human Nature* (Ithaca, NY: Cornell University Press, 1978). While living in London in 2000 I had many occasions to meet with her, and I owe her a great deal.

10. Wolves

1 In the Central Park jogger case the media referred to the men who attacked the woman as a "pack of wolves" ("Wolf's Pack Prey," *New York Daily News*, April 21, 1989).

2 See Rick McIntyre, *War Against the Wolf: America's Campaign to Exterminate the Wolf* (Stillwater, MN: Voyageur Press, 1995).

3 See Douglas W. Smith and Gary Ferguson, *Decade of the Wolf: Returning the Wild to Yellowstone* (Guilford, CT: Lyons Press, 2006). At present there are 120

wolves in Yellowstone. They had not been there for seventy-five years. The most authoritative book on the wolf remains David Mech's *The Wolf* (New York: Doubleday, 1970). See too his more recent book, edited with Luigi Boitani: *Wolves: Behavior, Ecology, and Conservation* (Chicago: University of Chicago Press, 2003). If I am not mistaken, it was Mech who was the first to point out that wolves did not deserve their reputation for danger to humans.

4 See Jon T. Coleman, *Vicious: Wolves and Men in America* (New Haven: Yale University Press, 2004). "In their stories, Euro-American colonists invented and broadcast a vision of wolves as threats to human safety. They then modeled their behavior on the ferocity they perceived in wolves. Thus folk-lore explains not only why humans destroyed wolves but why they did so with such cruel enthusiasm" (106).

5 For Norway, see the essay "Danger from Wolves," available online: http://en.wikipedia.org/wiki/Wolf_attacks_on_humans, fn. 57.

6 See Bruce Weide, "Wolf Attack!" *Wild Sentry Newsletter* 31 (Spring 2001), www.wildsentry.org/WolfAttack.html.

11. Kindness?

1 I am well aware of the fact that Primo Levi, Alexander Solzhenitsyn, and Anne Frank, who all gave voice to similar sentiments, are far better placed than I am to make such a judgment: they have been into the bowels of hell. So I take their words very seriously.

2 The most famous article about altruism was written by Robert Trivers when he was a graduate student at Harvard: "The Evolution of Reciprocal Altruism," *Quarterly Review of Biology* 46 (1971): 35–57. See his later formulation in 1985 in the collection of his essays *Social Evolution* (Menlo Park, CA: Benjamin/Cummings). I am grateful to him for several e-mail discussions on this topic. See too Lee Alan Dugatkin, *The Altruism Equation: 7 Scientists Search for the Origins of Goodness* (Princeton, NJ: Princeton University Press, 2006). I also enjoyed his 2011 book *The Prince of Evolution: Peter Kropotkin's Adventures in Science and Politics* (self-published), for Kropotkin's views are very similar to my own.

3 Cf. the old Arabic saying: "Me and my brother against my cousin; me, my brother, and my cousin against the stranger." But does this really correspond to anyone's experience today?

4 Richard D. Alexander, *Darwinism and Human Affairs* (Seattle: University of Washington Press, 1979), 271. See too his *Biology of Moral Systems* (New

York: Aldine de Gruyter, 1987). I have benefitted from a discussion of these issues with him.

5 George C. Williams, "Mother Nature Is a Wicked Old Witch," in *Evolutionary Ethics*, ed. Matthew H. Nitecki and Doris V. Nitecki (Albany: State University of New York Press, 1993).

6 T. H. Huxley, *Evolution and Ethics, with New Essays on Its Victorian and Sociobiological Context by James Paradis and George C. Williams* (Princeton, NJ: Princeton University Press, 1989).

7 Anna Freud, *The Ego and the Mechanisms of Defence*, tr. Cecil Baines (London: Hogarth Press, 1948). May I add here that the defense Anna Freud calls "identification with the aggressor" was actually one already used with that exact name by Sandor Ferenczi in a paper, "The Confusion of Tongues between Adults and the Child," which he read to the International Psycho-Analytical Association yearly meeting in 1932 in Wiesbaden, at which Anna Freud was present. He spoke there of the fact that children who are sexually abused often identify and protect the perpetrator, something still of immense value today.

8 For readers interested in going into more depth on this matter, see my book *The Assault on Truth: Freud's Suppression of the Seduction Theory* (New York: Farrar, Straus and Giroux, 1984).

9 Both quotes come from Dugatkin, *The Altruism Equation*, 62.

10 In his preface to Ronald Clark, *The Life and Work of J. B. S. Haldane* (Oxford: Oxford University Press, 1968).

12. A Billion Acts of Kindness

1 Kogon, a Christian survivor of Buchenwald, where he spent six years, gave witness at the Buchenwald trial in 1947.

2 Stephen Jay Gould, *I Have Landed: The End of a Beginning in Natural History* (New York: Harmony, 2002), 400.

3 Jeremy Rifkin, *The Empathic Civilization: The Race to Global Consciousness in a World in Crisis* (New York: Jeremy P. Tarcher, 2009).

4 I take this from *The Diary of Anne Frank: The Critical Edition*, prepared by the Netherlands State Institute for War Documentation (New York: Doubleday, 1989). This indispensable text contains a summary of the report by the State Forensic Science Laboratory of the Ministry of Justice compiled by H. J. J. Hardy, authenticating the diary, and also giving the information I use about the German policeman who arrested the group in the Annex.

Epilogue: Elephant Trauma and the Promise of a Better World

1 Steven C. Amstrup, Ian Stirling, Tom S. Smith, Craig Perham, and Gregory W. Thiemann, "Recent Observations of Intraspecific Predation and Cannibalism Among Polar Bears in the Southern Beaufort Sea," *Polar Biology*, 2006.

2 See D. G. Dutton, E. O. Boyanowsky, and M. H. Bond, "Extreme Mass Homicide: From Military Massacre to Genocide," *Aggression and Violent Behavior* 10 (2005): 437–73.

3 See N. A. Nikam and Richard McKeon, *The Edicts of Asoka* (Chicago: University of Chicago Press, 1959). See too Vincent A. Smith, *Asoka: The Buddhist Emperor of India*, 3rd ed. (Oxford: Clarendon Press, 1920), and, most important, *Romila Thapar, Aśoka at the Decline of the Mauryas*, 3rd ed. (Oxford India Perennials, 1997).

Appendix VI: The Problem with Pinker on the Problem of Human Violence

1 See the excellent review by John Gray, "Delusions of Peace," *Prospect* 187 (September 21, 2011).

2 This is a very conservative estimate. Sarah Staveteig has an article, "How Many Persons in East Timor Went 'Missing' During the Indonesia Occupation? Results from Indirect Estimates," (International Institute for Applied Systems Analysis Interim Reports, January 31, 2007), in which she writes that her best estimate of excess mortality is 204,000 people, or nearly a third of the entire population.

3 Robert Knox Dentan, *The Semai: A Nonviolent People of Malaya* (New York: Holt, Rinehart and Winston, 1968).

4 Here is what Boehm writes in "Ancestral Hierarchy and Conflict," *Science*, May 18, 2012: "The contemporary humans most appropriate for this evolutionary analysis are mobile hunter-gatherers who continue the 'culturally modern' behaviors associated with anatomically modern humans starting about 45,000 years ago in the Late Pleistocene. Many scholars have arbitrarily written off these potential exemplars because in recent times they have been so politically 'marginalized'; however, I suggest that Late Pleistocene populations were similarly marginalized because of climate shifts. Thus, contemporary foragers—but just those who are economically and culturally independent and isolated from domestication and modern commerce—in fact are likely exemplars for what culturally modern humans were doing in the Late Pleistocene."

BIBLIOGRAPHY

An asterisk designates a work that was particularly helpful in writing this book.

Archer, John. *The Behavioural Biology of Aggression.* Cambridge Studies in Behavioural Biology. Cambridge: Cambridge University Press, 1988.

Balibar, Etienne, and Immanuel Wallerstein. *Race, Nation, Class: Ambiguous Identities.* London: Verso, 1991.

Barash, David P., ed. *Understanding Violence.* Boston: Allyn and Bacon, 2001. (Useful anthology.)

Barlow, George W., and James Silverberg, eds. *Sociobiology: Beyond Nature/ Nurture? Reports, Definitions and Debate.* Boulder, CO: Westview Press, 1980.

Baron, Robert A., and Deborah R. Richardson. *Human Aggression.* 2nd ed. New York: Plenum Press, 1994.

Baum, Steven K. *The Psychology of Genocide: Perpetrators, Bystanders, and Rescuers.* Cambridge: Cambridge University Press, 2008.

Baumeister, Roy F. *Evil: Inside Human Violence and Cruelty.* New York: W. H. Freeman, 1997.

Bobbitt, Philip. *The Shield of Achilles: War, Peace, and the Course of History.* New York: Random House, 2003.

Bolgiano, Chris. *Mountain Lion: An Unnatural History of Pumas and People.* Mechanicsburg, PA: Stockpole Books, 2001.

Borofsky, Robert. *Yanomami: The Fierce Controversy and What We Can Learn from It.* Los Angeles: University of California Press, 2005.

Cullather, Nick. *Secret History: The CIA's Classified Account of Its Operations in Guatemala, 1952–1954.* Palo Alto, CA: Stanford University Press, 1999.

Daly, Martin, and Margo Wilson. *Homicide.* New Brunswick, NJ: Transaction, 1988.

Dower, John W. *Cultures of War: Pearl Harbor, Hiroshima, 9-11, Iraq.* New York: W. W. Norton & Company, 2010.

Droescher, Vitus B. *They Love and Kill: Sex, Sympathy and Aggression in Courtship and Mating.* New York: E. P. Dutton, 1976.

Ehrenreich, Barbara. *Blood Rites: Origins and History of the Passions of War.* New York: Henry Holt, 1997.

Eibl-Eibesfeldt, Irenaus, and Frank Kemp Salter, eds. *Indoctrinability, Ideology, and Warfare: Evolutionary Perspectives.* New York: Berghahn Books, 1998.

Ewer, R. F. *The Carnivores.* Ithaca, NY: Cornell University Press, 1973.

Feagin, Joe R., and Clairece Booher Feagin. *Racial and Ethnic Relations.* 6th ed. Englewood Cliffs, NJ: Prentice Hall, 1999.

Fox, James Alan, and Jack Levin. *The Will to Kill: Explaining Senseless Murder.* Boston: Pearson, 2006.

Fox, Robin. *The Violent Imagination.* New Brunswick, NJ: Rutgers University Press, 1989.

Fredrickson, George M. *The Comparative Imagination: On the History of Racism, Nationalism, and Social Movements.* Berkeley: University of California Press, 2000.

Gellner, Ernest. *Nations and Nationalism.* Ithaca, NY: Cornell University Press, 1983.

Goldberg, Carl. *The Evil We Do: The Psychoanalysis of Destructive People.* Amherst, NY: Prometheus Books, 2000.

Hallie, Philip P. *Cruelty.* Rev. ed. Middletown, CT: Wesleyan University Press, 1982 [1969].

Hinde, Robert A., and Helen E. Watson, eds. *War: A Cruel Necessity: The Bases of Institutionalized Violence.* London: I. B. Tauris, 1995.

Horowitz, Donald L. *Ethnic Groups in Conflict.* 2nd ed. Berkeley: University of California Press, 2000.

Ives, Richard. *Of Tigers and Men: Entering the Age of Extinction.* New York: Doubleday, 1996.

Judah, Tim. *Kosovo: War and Revenge.* New Haven: Yale University Press, 2002.

Keegan, John. *A History of Warfare.* New York: Alfred A. Knopf, 1993.

Kelly, Raymond C. *Warless Societies and the Origin of War.* Ann Arbor: University of Michigan Press, 2002.

Klama, John. *Aggression: Conflict in Animals and Humans Reconsidered.* London: Longman, 1988.

Kressel, Neil. J. *Mass Hate: The Global Rise of Genocide and Terror.* New York: Plenum Press, 1996.

Levi, Primo. *If This Is a Man.* New York: Orion Press, 1959. (Later reprinted as *Survival in Auschwitz.*)

Levinas, Emmanuel. *Humanism of the Other.* Trans. Nidra Poller. Introduction by Richard A. Cohen. Chicago: University of Illinois Press, 2006.

Logan, Kenneth, and Linda Sweanor: *Desert Puma: Evolutionary Ecology of an Enduring Carnivore.* Foreword by Maurice G. Hornocker. Washington, D.C.: Island Press, 2001.

Marks, Jonathan. *What It Means to Be 98% Chimpanzee: Apes, People, and Their Genes.* Berkeley: University of California Press, 2002.

Matthews, L. Harrison. "Overt Fighting in Mammals." In *The Natural History of Aggression*, ed. J. D. Carthy and F. J. Ebling, 23–38. Institute of Biology Symposia Number 13. London: Academic Press, 1964. (Discussion by Huxley, Lorenz.)

McGowan, Christopher. *The Raptor and the Lamb: Predators and Prey in the Living World.* London: Penguin, 1997.

Menatory, Anne. *The Art of Being a Wolf.* New York: Barnes and Noble, 2004.

*Miller, Arthur G. "What Can the Milgram Obedience Experiments Tell Us About the Holocaust?" In *The Social Psychology of Good and Evil*, ed. Arthur G. Miller, 193–239. New York: Guilford Press, 2004.

Morrow, Lance. *Evil: An Investigation.* New York: Basic Books, 2003.

Naimark, Norman M. *Fires of Hatred: Ethnic Cleansing in Twentieth-Century Europe.* Cambridge, MA: Harvard University Press, 2001.

Neiman, Susan. *Evil: An Alternative History of Philosophy.* Princeton: Princeton University Press, 2002.

Nicosia, Francis R., and Jonathan Huener, eds. *Medicine and Medical Ethics in Nazi Germany.* Oxford: Berghahn Books, 2002.

Olson, Steve. *Mapping Human History: Genes, Races, and Our Common Origins.* Boston: Houghton Mifflin, 2002.

Packer, Craig. *Into Africa.* Chicago: University of Chicago Press, 1994.

Padel, Ruth. *Tigers in Red Weather.* London: Little, Brown, 2005.

Perlmutter, Philip. *Legacy of Hate: A Short History of Ethnic, Religious, and Racial Prejudice in America.* London: M. E. Sharpe, 1999.

Pincus, Jonathan H. *Base Instincts: What Makes Killers Kill?* New York: W. W. Norton & Company, 2002.

*Quammen, David. *Monster of God: The Man-Eating Predator in the Jungles of History and the Mind.* New York: W. W. Norton, 2003.

Raffles, Hugh. *Insectopedia.* New York: Pantheon Books, 2010.

Ricciuti, Edward R. *Killer Animals: Shocking True Stories of Deadly Conflicts Between Humans and Animals.* Guilford, CT: Lyons Press, 2003.

Rifkin, Jeremy. *The Empathic Civilization: The Race to Global Consciousness in a World in Crisis.* New York: Penguin, 2009.

Schaller, George B. *The Serengeti Lion: A Study of Predator-Prey Relations.* Chicago: University of Chicago Press, 1972.

Schlink, Bernhard. *Guilt About the Past.* Toronto: University of Queensland Press, 2009.

Shaw, Harley. *Soul Among Lions: The Cougar as Peaceful Adversary.* Tucson: University of Arizona Press, 2000.

Silverberg, James, and J. Patrick Gray, eds. *Aggression and Peacefulness in Humans and Other Primates.* New York: Oxford University Press, 1992.

Singh, Arjun. *Tiger! Tiger!* London: Jonathan Cape, 1984.

Smaje, Chris. *Natural Hierarchies: The Historical Sociology of Race and Caste.* London: Blackwell, 2000.

Smith, David Livingstone. *Less than Human: Why We Demean, Enslave, and Exterminate Others.* New York: St. Martin's Press, 2011.

*Stanford, Craig. *Significant Others: The Ape-Human Continuum and the Quest for Human Nature.* New York: Basic Books, 2001.

*Sussman, Robert W., and Donna Hart. *Man the Hunted: Primates, Predators, and Human Evolution.* Boulder, CO: Westview, 2005.

*Totten, Samuel, William S. Parsons, and Israel W. Charny, eds. *Century of Genocide: Critical Essays and Eyewitness Accounts.* 2nd ed. New York: Routledge, 2004.

Valentino, Benjamin A. *Final Solutions: Mass Killing and Genocide in the 20th Century.* Ithaca, NY: Cornell University Press, 2004. (See chapter on Guatemala.)

Wainwright, Robert, and Paola Totaro. *Born or Bred: Martin Bryant: The Making of a Mass Murderer.* Sydney: Fairfax Books, 2009.

*Woods, Vanessa. *Bonobo Handshake: A Memoir of Love and Adventure in the Congo.* New York: Penguin, 2010.

Wrangham, Richard, and Dale Peterson. *Demonic Males: Apes and the Origins of Human Violence.* Boston: Houghton Mifflin, 1996.

Zahn, Gordon. *In Solitary Witness: The Life and Death of Franz Jaegerstaetter.* New York: Holt, Rinehart and Winston, 1964.

*Zajonc, R. B. "The Zoomorphism of Human Collective Violence." In *Understanding Genocide: The Social Psychology of the Holocaust,* ed. Leonard S. Newman and Ralph Erber, 222–38. New York: Oxford University Press, 2002. (Discussion of chimp wars.)

INDEX

A Note on the Author

JEFFREY MOUSSAIEFF MASSON is a former psychoanalyst who was, briefly, director of the Freud Archives. He has taught the history of psychoanalysis and journalistic ethics at the University of Toronto and the University of Michigan. At present he is an honorary research associate in the department of philosophy and sociology at the University of Auckland in New Zealand. He is the author of numerous books, most recently *Dogs Make Us Human*, and bestselling books on animal emotions, including *Dogs Never Lie About Love*, *When Elephants Weep*, and *The Dog Who Couldn't Stop Loving*. Visit his website at www.jeffreymasson.com.